Āyurveda & The Feminine

Heal your inner Goddess and claim your power back with this step by step guide to Vedic healing through Āyurveda, yoga, and other ancient rituals and practices.

By Monica B Groover

DISCLAIMER: This book and its information is not intended to prevent, cure, or diagnose any issues, imbalances, or diseases.

Āyurveda and its practitioners are not allowed to treat, cure, prevent, or diagnose any disease.

All information presented is for educational and informational purposes only.

Part of the artwork on the front cover has been used with permission from Śyāmarāṇī from her painting Sevākuñja, where the Divine Feminine is being served.

ISBN: 978-1-7350228-5-7

Maṅgalācaraṇa

(Invocation mantras to bless the writer of this book, the book itself and the readers)

oṁ ajñāna-timirāndhasya jñānāñjana-śalākayā
cakṣur unmīlitaṁ yena tasmai śrī-gurave namaḥ

I was born in the darkest ignorance, and my spiritual master Śrīla Bhaktivedānta Nārāyaṇa Mahārāja opened my eyes with the torch of knowledge. I offer my respectful obeisances unto him.

nārāyaṇaṁ namaskṛtya naraṁ caiva narottamam
devīṁ sarasvatīṁ vyasaṁ tato jayam udīrayet

I offer respectful obeisances unto the Divine, Nārāyaṇa, unto Nara-Nārāyaṇa Ṛṣi, the supermost human being, unto Mother Sarasvatī, the goddess of learning, and unto Śrīla Vyāsadeva.

kastūrī-tilakaṁ lalāṭa-paṭale vakṣaḥ-sthale kaustubhaṁ
nāsāgre nava-mauktikaṁ kara-tale veṇuṁ kare kaṅkaṇam
sarvāṅge hari-candanaṁ sulalitaṁ kaṇṭhe ca muktāvaliṁ
gopa-strī pariveṣṭito vijayate gopāla-cūḍāmaṇiḥ

Oh Gopāla, Krishna, who wears sacred symbols made by kasturi (musk) on his forehead, and who wears the Kaustubha crystal on his chest; you wear a pearl on your nose, and your hands hold a flute. Your arms are wearing bracelets. You are anointed with sandalwood paste. There are denizens of Goloka surrounding you. You are the protector of cows, animals, and all women. Please accept my salutations and protect us all who are weak and oppressed.

namāmi dhanvantarim ādi-devaṁ
surāsurair vandita-pada-padmam
lokair jarā-rug-bhaya-mṛtyu-nāśaṁ
dhātāram īśaṁ vividhauṣadhīnām

Oh Krishna, Oh Vishnu, Oh Nārāyaṇa, you manifest Lord Dhanvantari - the presiding deity of Āyurveda, healing, and of all healing herbs. I salute you. Please give me your blessing and medicine to help me become a medium to the community. You are the vaidya. I am a humble servant. Please provide your grace to the world just like you even give your blessing to devas (angels) and asuras.

sarva-maṅgala-māṅgalye śive sarvārtha-sādhike
śaraṇye tryambake gauri nārāyaṇi namo 'stu te

Oh Goddess Nārāyaṇī, one who is mother nature herself, also called Ambikā and Gaurī — you are all-auspicious and fulfill the desires of devotees.

Oh Mother - You preside over the running of the material world as Krishna's śakti (potency), as Mahāmāyā, the illusory power. You are the greatest illusionist. You are known as Yogamāyā, the goddess of mysticism and illusion, the giver of devotion. Please bestow śakti, bhakti, and devotion for Krishna to me. Dearest Yogamāyā, you manifest as Annapurṇā, the presiding deity of grains. As Śītalā Devī, you demonstrate yourself as the destroyer of disease and protector of small children, holding a pot of herbs in one hand and a broom in another.

You showered your blessings on me and came to me in a dream. You are the one writing this book through me.

Oh wife of Śaṅkara, please forgive my errors and accept this book as an offering to your feet.

praṇamya śirasā devaṁ gaurī-putraṁ vināyakam
bhaktāvāsaṁ smaren nityam āyuṣkāmārtha-siddhaye

Oh Gaṇeśa, son of Gaurī, please accept my salutations. You are the protector of the devotees, and help them with long life, health, and fulfillment of desires. Please help us in removing obstacles.

Acknowledgments

My acknowledgments, prayers, and a thousand praṇāms to my spiritual master, Śrīla Bhaktivedānta Nārāyaṇa Mahārāja.

Please reveal the light of knowledge and remove my darkness by your causeless mercy in front of my eyes, and for those who read this book.

I give my praṇāms to my first Guru and father - Sri Raj Baldev, whose tales of the divine Lord Vishnu gave me life from childhood.

I offer my acknowledgments and love to my dearest husband, śikṣā-guru, spiritual guide, and partner Paṇḍita Atul Krishna.

My acknowledgment and praṇāms to Śri Rāmcandra Prabhu and Rāgalekha didi, my godbrother and godsister, who have inspired me through the years.

I thank my mother, brother, and my sons Kush and Eshan.

Special thanks and salutations to Śyāmarāṇī didi for allowing me to use the front page image of Sevākuñja Rādhā, (*made for Śrīla Nārāyaṇa Mahārāja),* and for sharing her wisdom, for her beautiful art, and for encouraging me to get my books out.

Thank you, Dr. Aparna Dandekar, for your support.

Thank you to my beautiful and inspiring students.

I thank the spiritual and Āyurveda writers who have inspired me via their writings.

Thank you Pradeepa for being the yoga model.

Last but not least, thank you to all the students who have helped: Amy, Sarah, Leah, Krista, Heather and Fiona.

Contents

Maṅgalācaraṇa ... 1
Acknowledgments ... 3
Preface ... 9
Six essential steps for inner healing ... 19
Chapter 1: A quick introduction to Āyurveda ... 23
The origin of Āyurveda ... 23
Eight branches of Āyurveda ... 25
Mahābhūtās - the five elements ... 26
The three doṣas ... 28
Our original doṣa versus our current doṣa ... 30
Three states of mind ... 33
The ten opposing qualities or guṇas ... 35
The three types of woman ... 35
The vāta woman ... 37
The pitta woman ... 38
The kapha woman ... 40
What is a disease in Āyurveda? ... 42
Miseries, suffering, and karma ... 43
Internal ... 43
Other living beings ... 44
Act of nature ... 44
The karma ... 44
Four types of lifestyles ... 45
Importance of digestion and elimination ... 47
Parīkṣā (assessment and energetic biofeedback) ... 48
Fundamental Theories ... 50

Theory 1: Opposites attract 50
Theory 2: What is outside influences what's inside 51
Chapter 2: Āyurveda and women 53
Women's natural roles 53
Women in the workplace 55
The inner voice 61
Women throughout history 61
The yoni 63
The menstrual cycle 64
The menopause 65
Our inner layers (kośas) 65
The outermost layer 67
The energetic layer 68
The mind (manomaya-kośa) 68
The fourth layer (vijñānamaya-kośa) 69
The blissful layer (ānandamaya-kośa) 70
Chapter 3: Women are creatures of cycles 85
The cycle of the sun 87
The cycle of the moon 89
Āyurveda and the menstrual cycle 93
Pre-menstrual syndrome (PMS) 100
Herbs and diet for menstruation 101
Chapter 4: The menopause 105
Śakti 109
The moon and its importance for women 112
Chapter 5: Pregnancy and post partum care 115
Āyurveda and pregnancy 115
Conception and fertility 117

Signs of conception 120
Signs of pregnancy (garbha-lakṣaṇas) 121
Caring in the first trimester 121
First month 122
Second month 124
Third month 125
The second trimester 126
The last trimester 127
Post childbirth 128
Chapter 6: Introduction to Vāstu 131
Chapter 7: Mantras and meditation 139
The power of sound 139
Invoking feminine divine in your altar or garden 143
The practice of meditation 148
The object of meditation 153
Chapter 8: Communing with nature through herbs 157
Chapter 9: Ancient wisdom and modern nutrition 167
Buy prāṇa infused local produce 169
Where do frozen foods and leftovers fit in? 170
Sattva, rajas and tamas diet 171
Plant-based diet 172
Importance of detoxification 176
Chapter 10: Yoga for Women 185
Nāḍīs: Energetic channels of our body 186
The seven chakras 188
Āsanas 189
Crown chakra 190
The "third eye" chakra 191

Throat chakra 192
Heart chakra 194
Stomach chakra 195
Sacral chakra 196
Root chakra 197
Questionnaire 199
Vāta woman profile 200
Pitta woman profile 203
Kapha woman profile 205
Āyurvedic kitchen 209
About the author 215

Preface

My spiritual name is Manjulali, and I will refer to myself as such in the book. This book is a culmination of my own personal, mystical, and sacred journey in the last twenty years. Here is a little background information about me.

When I was small, my mother ran a successful printing press in south Delhi. This was the seventies, and this was unheard of at that time in India: a woman business owner with employees.

My father worked from home. He'd pick me up from school and inundate me with stories of Hindu Gods and Goddesses. I would learn lessons about life, healing through mantras, Vedic astrology, meditation, and herbs. He taught me sacred sounds. The board games we played at home were séance boards. (I thought it was fake and a game — I am not so sure now).

He taught me about higher entities and how to receive messages from them. We would prepare lehyam (Āyurvedic jam) with many bitter and tonic herbs and offer it to the sun.

We would also make sun tea in a copper pot by submitting water to the sun with mantras. We would do rituals for the moon with water in a crystal or silver jar.

Unbeknownst to me, this time was going to change the course of my life. I didn't know it at the time, but this was my alternative schooling in the mystical arts and Vedic healing.

While other girls played with toys, I pretended to be a healer and spiritualist, mixing my herbs with mantras. Our house in Delhi was behind a famous hiking trail forest called Deer Park.

I would go to Deer Park almost every single morning before school. I would place my deities, collect flowers, check out the fantastic array of plants and trees, and pretend I was a healer and a forest spirit.

I would meditate every single day without fail, from age six onwards.

When I was ten years old, I sat down to do my daily meditation in lotus pose. I am told that I went into a state of trance for many hours when I sat on my father's meditation mat. I have some prominent memories of what I experienced in 4K, along with sights, smells, and sounds.

When I opened my eyes, only a few seconds had passed for me. I saw my parents and our family doctor trying to revive me. For them, it had been many hours; long enough to summon doctors to revive me from my state of trance.

That is a delicious memory, but a story for another time.

After this "trance" incident, I developed an uncanny sense of intuition and some psychic abilities.

At ten, I didn't know what those abilities were and never nurtured them. I just knew that I sometimes knew things before they happened. I could sense good or bad "stuff." That's it.

I did not fully embrace my intuitive and psychic abilities until my twenties.

Since I have embraced the intuitive in me, so much knowledge, divine communication, and blessings have flowed from the "other" side. I honestly don't know what the other side is. I call it a different dimension.

I genuinely believe all of us have a "third eye" sense and some intuition. When we don't use it, we lose it.

I grew up and studied in Delhi, India, and finished my undergraduate studies in the same city.

I lived and studied in England for some years in the late nineties. This was a time of some anxiety and fundamental change in me.

I met one of my spiritual guides in London who introduced me to my spiritual master, Śrīla Bhaktivedānta Nārāyaṇa Mahārāja.

When I met my spiritual master, I had no life goals and was a confused 23 years old. I viewed the sufferings in the world and had a thousand philosophical questions about life and suffering.

My guru gave me the name Manjulali Dasi. Manjulali is the name of a young "servitor" of the Supreme Goddess. Dasi means to serve. (One who serves the servant)

The life of a strict Vaishnavite (one who worships Vishnu) with emphasis on Vedic studies was precisely what I needed at that time.

I studied Bhagavad Gītā, yoga texts, Bhāgavata Purāṇa, Āyurvedic saṁhitās, and texts. I poured myself into this strict lifestyle for the next six years.

The devotees were expected to wake up a few hours before dawn for morning spiritual activities that included meditation, studying scriptures, and kirtan. I must admit that getting up at 4 am was hard for me. It was also the best time to get significant studies and meditation accomplished.

The daily routine included studying Vedic scriptures as well as daily chanting. While pursuing my studies, I maintained myself with a part-time job on the side while living at home and learning the ways of the ashram on weekends.

I gradually embraced spiritual life 100%, to the dismay of my mother, who had hoped I would be a medical doctor.

I became a strict vegetarian and started following a sādhana of food, mantras, and meditation, as prescribed by the Vedas and Gauḍīya vedāntic philosophy. It was so exciting to me that food was 'Brahman' or God itself. Also, food had to be offered and empowered so it could give us prāṇa and heal our hearts, besides giving us physical strength.

I worked two or three days a week as a makeup artist for television programs. This was a part-time job on the side to make some money, while trying to follow the rules of a female initiate of the ashram during weekends and holidays.

It was hard to be a single woman and a female initiate. A primarily monastic Gauḍīya Vaiṣṇava institution expected Indian women usually to present themselves with a good husband in tow, or to be blazingly intelligent and humble, and to always take a back seat to the men.

Even in the ashram, I was a natural nonconformist. That earned me a little bit of a feminist reputation, which I wore as a badge of honor.

One English godbrother with a medical condition lived in the ashram at that time. He dabbled in many alternative forms of healing and introduced his new hobby to me.

My interest in Āyurvedic healing grew tremendously due to his medical condition. Eventually, this inspired me to study the Āyurvedic texts under masters and gurus who had digested the teachings.

I tried everything including crystals, mantras, magnet therapy, and reiki. I brewed kombucha in the nineties when no one had heard of it.

I made my lipsticks with ghee, licorice, and kumkum powder. I made anjana (black kohl called kajal used for eye makeup) with ghee wicks. I made blush powder with rose petals and arrowroot. (I had a part-time job as a makeup artist for television actors.)

This was also the time in the late nineties that I became seriously interested in Āyurveda and tried Āyurvedic herbal formulations and spiritual fasting.

Being a modern Vaishnavite *(someone who worships Krishna, or Vishnu, the creator*) and lacking conformist attitude, I struggled with the patriarchal and conservative atmosphere of the ashram.

However, I was still able to absorb the beautiful teachings and atmosphere.

I was encouraged by incredible spiritual leaders in New Delhi and Vrindavan, who continue to inspire both men and women to take up spiritual Vedic life.

At some point, I needed to make money and was under pressure from my parents to continue my studies at the University. It was back to student life for me, and the ashram became a part-time endeavor for when I had time.

Some years later, I met my husband-to-be. We got married.

Eventually, I moved from India to the United States. I began the traditional householder's life with a job, children, home, and working to make money.

Over time, the sādhanas and practices completely took a back seat.

However, as I have gone through my sacred journey of physical acceptance, mental wisdom, and spiritual healing, I have come to understand who I am and my relationship with mother nature.

I am also at peace with the larger Kapha-size body, instead of hating myself for being big. *(This is something society imposes on us: if women are overweight, it must be our fault.)*

I feel grateful for the teachings that I have been blessed with and want to share it with others.

I have been on a continuous cycle of healing myself with spiritual and Vedic practices, then falling off the bandwagon only to get back on it again and again.

As I have been on a process of food sādhana and Āyurvedic healing, somehow women have been drawn to me, and inadvertently I have helped ladies from India, Mexico, and Europe as well as the USA.

I have been attempting to guide them with subtle changes in their physical, astral, and spiritual bodies. This guidance is to support pregnancy, postpartum, perimenopause or post-menopause, or stress.

I started teaching Āyurveda and Vedic arts along with my husband Atul Krishna a decade ago to help my clients. There was no business plan for our school.

It was completely organic. I had one intention.

Help others. That's it.

Despite lack of business loans and no business plan, no advertising and no budget, the school we started took off, and the rest, as they say, is history.

My school and my Āyurveda practice have been blessed by providence with abundance, beautiful teachers, and students.

I am so grateful to all the students and lovely women who have approached me in the last decade or so.

I am not writing this book because I have had an epiphany about how to make womankind happy and healed, nor have I lost 100 pounds.

In fact, I struggle to keep my daily routine, seasonal routine, Āyurvedic diet plans, and still very much have my weight issues. What I have learned is that when we fall off the bandwagon, we must get back on it and be satisfied with the lemons we have been given. (Learn to make lemonade, as they say).

Using the spiritual and Āyurveda teachings, I manage to stay on life's treadmill and if I fall down, I get back on it again and again. The goal is to somehow balance everything — life, family, husband, children, running the school, running my Āyurveda Center, and teaching — while maintaining my meditation and healing practices, and living a life of service.

During the last twelve years in the United States, through my Āyurveda practice, I have met thousands of women, and they have benefited from Āyurveda, yoga therapy, mantras, and crystals.

Whether an imbalance stems from divorce, emotional trauma, or a physical imbalance, the ancient healing therapies, Āyurveda, and vegetarian Vedic diet seem to have supported so many ladies. I wanted to share this with the world.

In this book, you will learn about herbs, nutrition, and your Āyurvedic body type. You will learn about the power of sounds and chants, invoking higher feminine energy to bring peace, healing, and abundance in your life.

We will use ancient rituals to summon the Feminine Divine by establishing an altar, a special place to collect blessings and abundance.

We will also talk about Āyurveda, Āyurvedic herbs and nutrition, women's cycles that include the menstrual cycle, PMS, menopause, pregnancy and antepartum, as well as some practical Āyurvedic tips.

This book is also a culmination of my mystical and fantastic journey and submitted to all you beautiful women out there with humility and respect.

Everything is personal, subjective, and Vedic and has pearls of Āyurvedic wisdom interspersed.

I didn't want this book to be just about Āyurveda. I want to talk about spiritual and women's relationships with this knowledge. Thus I have tried to keep the Āyurveda portion shorter than I am used to in my regular writings.

This is not a textbook of Āyurveda for women. It is a book about using healing advice from Āyurveda, ancient rituals, and Vedic teachings I have learned from my teachers.

I hope feminists are not offended by some of my own opinions. It's not my intention to offend anyone but to help.

Being a follower of Gauḍīya Vaiṣṇava philosophy, I have integrated the Gauḍīya Vaiṣṇava six-step process of achieving balance in health, weight, spirituality, family, food, and multi-tasking for women of all age groups. We use this process for spiritual advancement in our ashram. I have tweaked it a bit, as you will see.

You will see boxed notes that I call pearls of wisdom from ancient teachings throughout the book. There are also case studies and stories to make the instructions more palatable.

Last but not least, there are activities for you to do on your own. Take a notebook or a journal, for there is much information to download. Finish your activities in your journal.

Thank you for reading and giving your precious time to this book. I am so grateful to you for seeking this beautiful modality and alternative spiritual rituals and support.

I pray to my deities Rādhā-Kṛṣṇa, my teachers, and Mother Earth to bless this book, and whosoever reads it with sincerity should receive a positive change and blessings in their lives.

Love and Shanti,

Manjulali Dasi

PS: “Serving the Feminine Divine is my purpose.”

Six essential steps for inner healing

1. Become the observer
2. Acknowledge what you observe
3. Create intent
4. Cultivate new habits
5. Work on the mind (body follows)
6. Surrender

1. Become the observer
Become the observer. Observe yourself and your actions, your thoughts. Don't judge. Just observe. Understand your doṣa (vāta, pitta, and kapha) in your body and mind. Observe your weaknesses, strengths, reactions, and actions.

2. Acknowledge what you observe
Recognize and acknowledge our strengths and weaknesses, blessings, and understand that we make mistakes. Acknowledge what makes you who you are. Understand your inner voice. Understand that I am not this physical body, I am much more, and I have a spiritual duty to my ātmā (soul), my inner self. I need to nurture my body, mind, and soul to lead a better life. I am one complicated package.

3. Create intent
Create an intention and a general plan for your well-being.
Create an outline of objectives - what you want to do daily and monthly, and the changes you desire. The mind will start, and the body will follow. Take responsibility for your intention, and at the same time, put it out in the universe.

4. Cultivate new habits
Sattva is auspiciousness and truth, purity of the mind. Cultivate sāttvik activities. Cultivate a sāttvik plant-based diet if possible, as much as you can. Put pure sāttvik foods in your body, full of prāṇa, and cooked with love. Think pure thoughts. Associate with like-minded sāttvik people

5. Work on the mind (body follows)
Work on the mind first. Wherever the mind goes, the body follows. Meditate on your inner self. Become aware of the presence of Divine within, whether chanting, listening to music, working with a deity, or reading a book.

Use whatever tools help you in your journey: books, meditation, music, exercise, like-minded community, friends, and teachers. Prāṇāyama and yoga are helpful; use breathing techniques as a precursor to meditation, and use yoga as an exercise and fitness routine, as an adjunct to your routine.

6. Surrender
Understand that the universe has a plan for you in mysterious ways. Don't try to control things. Flow with it. Surrender.

These steps will be interwoven with activities distributed throughout the book. Some of these activities are at the end of chapters and others at the end of the book.

Chapter 1: A quick introduction to Āyurveda

Āyurveda (science of life) is a stand-alone holistic health modality from India steeped in condensed wisdom. It can take lifetimes to soak it all in.

Even though Āyurveda principles apply to everyone, in this book we will talk about specific healing therapies and modalities for women.

First, let's understand the origin of this beautiful modality.

Āyurveda is a multi-modality life science that deals with healing the body, mind, spirit, and consciousness.

The origin of Āyurveda

The origins of Āyurveda are mysterious, mystical, and considered mythical by some.

Thousands of years ago, sages in India brought this ancient knowledge of healing to the earth, according to Āyurvedic Texts.

However, as they are written in our primeval books, we consider the word of these ancient texts to be correct.

I am writing the origin of Āyurveda here, as told in the first section of one of the ancient writings in a book called Caraka Saṁhitā. *(One of the three essential books for Āyurveda practitioners).*

The story goes on how the knowledge of Āyurveda was passed from the Creator to angels in heavens. Then, the teachings were passed from heavenly beings to mystical sages. These sages brought the knowledge to planet earth and distributed it.

The story begins with the creator of the world called Brahmā, passing down the wisdom of healing to his son. You are probably wondering, who is Brahmā? In Vedic culture, there are three primary deities: Brahmā is the creator, Vishnu is the preserver, and Śiva is the destroyer. So, our story begins with Brahmā, the creator.

The ancient and divine knowledge of healing was hidden from the world. To spread the teachings, the creator Brahmā decided to instruct this ancient knowledge to one of his sons, Dakṣa Prajāpati.

Prajāpati chose to pass this knowledge onto the most qualified angels in the heavens: the celestial divine twins known as the Aśvini Kumāras. *(They are similar to the Proto-Indo-European Divine Twins, sons of Dyēus.)*

The Aśvini Kumāras are considered the physicians of the angels or devatas. Who was best qualified to receive these teachings from them? It was decided that Indra, the king of heaven, was best suited. The knowledge was passed to Indra. *(Indra is similar to Zeus, and carries a thunderbolt)*

A sage called Bharadvāja was visiting heaven. He had arrived from Earth.

Indra spent time with the sage Bharadvāja and passed down this healing knowledge to him.

In the next part of the story, this wisdom now travels to the planet Earth.

The sage Bharadvāja returned to planet earth armed with this knowledge and immediately shared it with his friend. His friend was another sage called Ātreya Punarvasu. Sage Ātreya is a significant character in the story of the origin of Āyurveda.

It was Ātreya's disciples that would write this knowledge that was passed in an oral tradition before their time.

Ātreya Punarvasu had many disciples, and he taught this ancient healing modality to all his disciples. All the disciples wrote down the teachings from their Master and took notes. These notes were taken on dried palm leaves. (Think scrolls).

One disciple of Ātreya called Agniveśa published these manuscripts. Agniveśa's manuscripts changed many forms over the years and became what is now called Caraka Saṁhitā, the most well-known text of Āyurveda.

Hence, Caraka Saṁhitā is generally regarded as one of the top three authoritative texts on Āyurveda, the other two being Suśruta Saṁhitā and Aṣṭāṅga Hṛdayam. Below, and later on, in this book, you will find information from these texts.

I have tried to present it in a way that is easy to understand. I decided to keep the Sanskrit names, for those readers who are motivated to study Āyurveda.

Eight branches of Āyurveda

Classically, Āyurveda had eight branches, out of which only some are practiced today in India.

The eight essential sub-specialties continue to be taught today, and they include:

- 1.Internal Medicine (kāya-cikitsā)
- 2.General Surgery (śalya-tantra)
- 3.Otorhinolaryngology or ENT (śālākya-tantra)
- 4.Pediatrics and Obstetrics / Gynecology (kaumāra-bhṛtya)
- 5.Psychiatry (bhūta-vidyā)
- 6.Toxicology (agaḍa-tantra)

- 7. Nutrition, Detoxification, and Rejuvenation (rasāyana-tantra)
- 8.Fertility and Virility (vājīkaraṇa)

Mahābhūtās - the five elements

Āyurveda believes that we are a spirit soul embodied in a physical body. We have a unique body-mind constitution called doṣa.

Āyurveda further believes that five basic components make up all organic and biomatter on our planet. These fundamental building blocks are called the mahābhūtas and are present in our DNA. The mahābhūtas are present in the base pairs of DNA in our genetic make-up, represented by the letters A, C, T, and G. They are also present in more gross forms in our physical body.

According to Āyurveda, everything is made up of these five building blocks of life, called the pañca-mahābhūtas.

These elements exist in the universe ranging from the cosmic scale down to the quantum scale, in macrocosm and microcosm.

These five elements make up the doṣas, our constitution.

SPACE

Space manifests as the quality of creativity, or as space within the ears or organs. For women, it manifests as feeling spaced out during hormonal disturbance, emotional disturbance, PMS, or pregnancy.

AIR

Air manifests as bloating, anxiety, or feeling ungrounded during the PMS and monthly cycle.

WATER

Water forms the liquid systems in the body like menstrual fluid, urine, and blood. In women, it expresses itself as tender breasts during PMS and monthly cycles.

EARTH

Earth is the structure of the body, and the ability to slow down and relax. In women, it may manifest as wanting to rest or relax during the monthly cycle or PMS. It may also manifest as feeling slow or less energetic.

The three dosas vāta, pitta, and kapha are made up of the five elements. I know this may sound confusing. Just try to think of it like this — whatever is the quality of air and space will be the quality of a vāta person. Once you go read about the ten opposing qualities (the twenty guṇas), this will make more sense.

In conclusion, these five elements will manifest themselves as doṣas in our bodies in particular configurations. These configurations are:

- Air and space dominate a vāta person and give them airy qualities of lightness and mobility.
- Fire and water dominant a pitta person and make them fiery and passionate.
- Earth and water exhibit themselves dominantly in a kapha person, and make them stable and nurturing.

These five elements do not manifest precisely in the same way in each person. In fact, they exhibit differences in the three-body types - vāta, pitta, and kapha - making each human being unique. Besides these basic differences, there are additional effects of the five elements during PMS, menstrual cycle, pregnancy, postpartum, or menopause.

The three doṣas

Doṣa can be translated as a weakness. A student asked me once, "Why would Āyurveda call someone's unique body-mind constitution a fault?"

This is how I explained it to her, "Earth has fault lines. Each fault line is a weak link, where all the seismic activity first manifests. Similarly, our doṣa is our fault line. Now, the first signs of imbalance or disease begin to manifest in this weak area, according to our doṣa. Our doṣa is our weakness in a pre-determined area where the disease may appear.

This weakness is what makes us special because when one area is weak, another is strong. Our doṣa influences our life choices, our mental and physical weaknesses, our strengths, our tastes, how we perceive heat and cold, our height, weight, the softness of our skin, and much, much more.

Our uniqueness is the very premise of Āyurveda. We are unique because we have a unique genetic code. From the Āyurvedic perspective, we also have a unique doṣa which shows in the way we handle disease, healing, life, and emotions. This is what makes us who we are.

The etymology of the Sanskrit word doṣa leads us to the concept of fault or inherent weakness. Just as earth experiences earthquakes around its fault lines, we may experience disease according to our doṣa. Our doṣa is our faultline.

Each doṣa is a psychophysical body-mind constitution which is unique to us. Some women can be dual doṣic, or a combination of two doṣas.

The permutation and combination of these five elements (pañca-mahābhūtas) in various patterns create the three doṣas. This, in turn, influences how we eat, how we look, and how we feel. It governs our mind, body, and spirit. The doṣas are responsible for our unique psychophysical constitution and reside in different locations within our bodies. The Greeks called them humors.

Let's review the configuration of the five elements and their relationship with doṣa that we learned in the previous page.

There are Sanskrit verses in ancient textbooks that sing the virtues of balanced doṣas. When vāta, pitta, and kapha are in a state of equilibrium, a human being will be healthy. When they are not in balance, it may result in an unwell physical, mental, and spiritual state.

Vāta doṣa is composed of air and space.
Pitta doṣa is composed of fire and water.
Kapha doṣa is composed of water and earth.

The Three Doṣas

Our original doṣa versus our current doṣa

Who doesn't love cute babies, be it humans or animals? Interestingly, in India, all expectant mothers are expected to look at healthy baby photos, be peaceful, and perform activities that bring happiness and comfort.

Comfort means different things to different people. Simple things can bring us joy. Active pursuits that can bring balance may include meditating in a garden, hiking on a mountain, hearing sounds of the sea, or smelling and seeing beautiful flowers.

From the Āyurvedic perspective, whatever an expectant mother eats, thinks, and sees will affect the body and mind of the developing fetus. It will impact the fetus's prakṛti.

Prakṛti translates as "my shape" or "my picture."

Prakṛti is the proportion of five elements in our constitution at the time of birth. The baby with the low weight may be considered vāta as her water and earth elements may be less. Perhaps her air and space elements are higher. This combination of increased air and space elements may also make her a light sleeper, and make her susceptible to constipation and dry skin. We would call her a vāta baby.

Comparatively, a kapha baby may be a very healthy nine pounds, chubby, and will sleep through anything. The kapha baby will tend to have oilier skin and may overdrink from his yummy mummy. Later on in life, the kapha baby may become overweight.

Prakṛti is how vāta, pitta, and kapha are quantified and manifested in our body and mind type, and is very much tied to our unique genetic code.

When my five-year-old asked me what original doṣa is, I explained it to him as an original photo of his energy. For example, a baby born with low weight has decreased water and earth element. Alternatively, a baby with a healthy nine- or ten-pound weight has increased water and earth.

The combination and proportions of vāta, pitta, and kapha are set at conception. This combination is the unique psychophysical makeup and functional habits of a person.

This original combination of vāta, pitta, and kapha, set at the time of conception and manifest after we are born is called prakṛti. The three doṣas exist in combination both in our body and and in our mind. This combination of the three doṣas keeps on developing till age 12 or 13. Hormones influence prakṛti after the onset of puberty.

Any deviation from the original or natural constitution is the current state of imbalance. This current state of inequality is not good. We call this imbalanced doṣa vikṛti.

To my little one, I explained vikṛti as the original photo of our energy changing if we don't eat plants, vegetables, and are always sad or angry.

Balancing the doṣas means balancing the vikṛti (present state of doṣas in the body) by soothing the aggravated doṣa. Consider your prakṛti (original constitution) and your dominant doṣa (vāta, pitta, or kapha) that is primarily responsible for your current state of imbalance (called vikṛti). Consider the attributes or qualities (guṇas) of this doṣa that are accumulated.

We use the opposite attributes of the doṣas to bring balance.

For example, if your pitta (heat) is high, you may experience symptoms of acidity, diarrhea, PMS, and skin issues. Additionally, endometriosis, hypertension, hot flashes, irritation, being critical, jealousy, and anger may manifest. Try to avoid heating foods, warming spices, overexertion, controlling emotions, and warm weather.

Here is another example: if your vāta (cold/dry) is high, you may experience dry skin/hair/nails, constipation, gas, back pain, and poor circulation. Additionally, headaches, insomnia, worry, mood swings, chronic fatigue, anxiety, and stress may manifest. Try avoiding cold weather, cold foods, and iced beverages; stay hydrated internally and externally.

Doṣas change with time, lifestyle, diet, and mindset. The changed doṣa is referred to as vikṛti. (literally translated as deformity of the original constitution).

There are two profiles that we need to determine in Āyurveda: the original constitution and the current constitution. At the end of this book are three forms — one each for vāta, pitta, and kapha. Please fill all THREE forms. Choose whatever applies to you on a scale of 1 to 5 on each of these forms. (Remember that we are a combination of ALL THREE doṣas).

The end of the book questionnaire will determine your original and current constitution or doṣa. The survey in which you get the maximum scores will determine your natural constitution and its deviation.

Three states of mind

Both yoga and Āyurveda practitioners believe in the three continuously changing states of consciousness. These are also called guṇas of the mind. These states are sattva, tamas, and rajas.

Think of a puppet or marionette. There are some ropes attached to the puppet, and the puppeteer makes it do whatever she likes. These three states continuously affect our choices and decisions.

Sattva is a state of purity.
Tamas is a state of lethargy.
Rajas is a state of passion.

The Three States of Mind

One of my students said to me once that it seems these three states of consciousness are connected to our primitive brain, which drives survival and instinct. Ultimately, all the choices our brain makes are influenced by a combination of these three states. These states are always changing according to our lifestyle, thinking, and even the food we eat.

My husband Atul gives an example of sattva, tamas, and rajas as primary colors. You can mix them and create millions of combinations. Human beings are a mix of these primary colors with millions of combinations. Let's look at these "colors" first.

Rajas is the state of GO. It is the state of movement and passion. Without this instinct, nothing would ever get done in the world. We move, we go out, we get things done. Without this state of rajas, all projects would remain unfinished, and nothing would ever get done.

Tamas is the state of STOP. It is a state of blissful ignorance and lethargy. It is a state of slowness vis-à-vis the movement and passion of rajas. Without this state of apathy, we'd never be able to wind down. We'd never be able to put out the lights and go to sleep. We need this as much as we need rajas.

Sattva is somewhere in the middle. The state of sattva makes a person happy where they are. Sattva dictates that we seek balance, peace, and higher truth. Sattva dictates that we accept a higher power. Sattva dictates that we should not be selfish. Without a state of sattva, we won't ever help our community, nor feel part of a whole.

For example, someone, mostly in a state of passion or rajas will make decisions based on emotion and their likes and dislikes. Everything is based on how they feel at that moment instead of intelligence. This person will always like to move, do something new. Their mind may be racing from one topic to another.

A person influenced by tamas or a state of lethargy will sit on a couch and watch movies, be too lazy to get out of their sweat pants, and just want to be left alone. Their mind may be sluggish and clouded.

Someone influenced by a state of sattva might be instinctively hygienic, thinks of others before herself, and is peaceful. Their mind is neither lazy nor racing.

Note that only higher beings can achieve a state of pure sattva or purity. Those of us from planet earth are always in a combination of the three states of mind, according to ancient texts.

Going back to the marionette analogy, think of the three ropes as sattva, tamas, and rajas - states that influence our perception and our choices, words, and actions. The good news is that our eating habits, the company we keep, and our lifestyle can produce an almost instant effect for the better.

The ten opposing qualities or guṇas

Each of the five elements gives its own merits to the doṣas. Let's quickly look at these ten opposing qualities.

Vāta is air and space; it has qualities of both air and space. (see below)
Pitta is fire and water; it exhibits qualities of water and fire. (see below).
Kapha women exhibit qualities of earth and water. (see below)

- **Qualities of Space** – Clear, Light, Soft, Subtle
- **Qualities of Air** – Mobile, Dry, Light, Cold, Subtle
- **Qualities of Fire** – Hot, Sharp, Light, Dry, Subtle
- **Qualities of Water** – Cold, Liquid, Soft, Oily, Unctuous
- **Qualities of Earth** – Heavy, Dull, Static, Dense, Hard, Gross

The Ten Qualities

The three types of woman

There are three doṣas - vāta, pitta, and kapha. Does this mean that there are three kinds of women? The answer is yes.

When women who have never heard of Āyurveda come to me, I end up not starting our conversation about their health imbalances, but by finding out who they are.

In my Women's Support Workshop, I ask women the question, "Who are you?" After the initial look of confusion, I hear a myriad of responses that reflect how a woman's sense of self is misidentified with her employment, her physical attributes, her environment, her nationality, her relationships, or her state of health and well-being.

Interestingly, the most popular response given by women remains, "I am a mother." However, by asking women the question, "Who are you?" I am asking them to reflect on their sense of identity, which is beyond what they do or how much they earn. I ask participants to see internally and to think about who they are inside as opposed to an external phenotype or lifestyle.

I am trying to determine their unique body, mind, and spirit composition. In other words, what's their doṣa.

A basic premise of Āyurveda includes that we are not this physical body that bleeds every month, has a yoni (vagina), and has biological needs. Underneath all that, we are spiritual beings - part of mother nature's śakti.

Let me reiterate that we are special, no matter what our body weight, color, height, or any external features. We are unique. We are beautiful. We are so distinctive that both our strengths and weaknesses are also unique. When we are weak in one area, we are more robust in another. The divine feminine has blessed us with two advantages for each of our failings. The weaknesses themselves are blessings in disguise.

For example, if a kapha woman is naturally overweight, she is also more stable, has higher immunity, and has a forgiving nature, provided she is balanced.

If a pitta woman has some skin issues or is naturally critical or gets riled easily, she also has double the strength and grit to persevere in hard times. If a balanced vāta woman tends to get ungrounded quickly, she can also return to her balance speedily and has this superhuman ability to multi-task and juggle and not drop the ball on anything.

Our doṣa influences our life choices, our mental and physical weakness, strengths, tastes, and how we perceive heat or cold. It influences our height, weight, the softness of our skin, and much more.

The qualities of these doṣas define our digestion, our monthly cycles, and influence childbirth and delivery as well as recovery. It also has a significant influence on what kind of menopause we may experience. (Yes, menopause in vāta, pitta, and kapha women will differ!) If you are a combination doṣa — let's say vāta and pitta — then both these doṣas will be a significant influence.

Let's learn a little bit more about this female triad of vāta, pitta, and kapha women. Let's understand how the qualities of air, space, fire, water, and earth make us so distinctive.

The vāta woman

Vāta is mobile. It is the energy of movement. It is responsible for all voluntary and involuntary movements, as well as any kind of circulation. Nothing can move without vāta. Vāta even governs our thoughts.

The combination of sattva and rajas (state of purity and movement) naturally influences the mind and body of vāta women.

Vāta is ruled by air and space, and these qualities are reflected in vāta woman imbalances.

The vāta is characterized by qualities of dryness, lightness, cold, and mobility.

Vāta women love to move, exercise, dance, sports activities, and even running around doing chores. They are creative and intuitive and quick to make body and mind changes. Vāta women are kind and sometimes have a hard time saying no to someone in need. They will end up helping everyone they can, till they burn out.

Sexually, a vāta woman may be playful, curious, and energetic.

They shine in professions that are creative like art, theatre, music, television. They are also attracted to charity and volunteer work.

When imbalanced, this "mobility" may sneak up on them as aches and pains that move from one body part to another. Fluctuation in the monthly cycle (heavy or light), blood pressure, and even variable appetite are some other manifestations of this mobile quality. One day a vāta person may be starving, and on another goes all day without a meal.

This mobile quality may also cause twitching.

The dryness is exhibited as dry skin, dry hair, constipation, dry hard stools, or vaginal dryness.

The lightness of vāta women may manifest as being slim, lightweight, and experiencing light bleeding in their monthly periods.

Emotionally it can also manifest as feeling imbalanced, lightheadedness, worrying, anxiety, forgetfulness, and even the urgent need to urinate. The mobile and light quality together make a recipe for moodiness and mood swings.

Often vāta women complain of cold hands and feet. They will be the first one to complain about air conditioning and demand a blanket.

The pitta woman

Pitta is the energy of transformation. It controls the metabolic functions inside the body. Pitta is sometimes called the energy of fire or agni. Pitta is heat and responsible for all kinds of transformation and metabolism. Whether it is cellular metabolism, our ability to turn ideas into actions, or the function of enzymes to convert and transform - it is all pitta.

Pitta is governed by a combination of some sattva, some tamas, and a lot of rajas (modes of goodness, ignorance, and passion).

Pitta women are ruled by fire and water.

Pitta women are smart, passionate, excitable, ambitious, critical (of themselves too), and impatient. They shine in professions that require grit, mental energy, and a great deal of intellect. Examples: scientist, accountant, engineer, mathematician, CEO, and managers.

The dominant qualities in a pitta woman are the same as those of fire and water. These include being warm to touch, hot temper, sharpness, light, liquid, spreading quickly, and oily.

Sexually, a pitta woman may be extremely passionate and blessed with a hyper sex drive. When imbalanced, the sex drive does get fizzled out.

When imbalanced, the anger and criticism rule along with heat and inflammation-related imbalances listed below.

The heat manifests as hot flashes and when not flashing, feeling warmer than usual, along with anger and night sweats. The pitta woman may also end up with acid reflux. The skin is warm and slightly reddish.

Inflammation is also a display of pitta's heat.

A pitta woman may also have sensitive reddish eyes. This photosensitivity in the eyes is also a display of heat quality.

The sharp quality in pitta may exhibit itself as a sharp wit, a smart-mouth who is always quick with a retort. This sharpness gives a keen intellect to pitta women. Adversely, the pain perception of a pitta woman is "Ouch!" They feel sharp pain.

Last but not least, acid reflux is also a manifestation of sharp quality.

The liquid and oily quality displays itself as oily skin with breakouts, heavy bleeding during the menstrual cycle, and even losing hair (on the head).

Pitta men tend to lose hair earlier on in life and have a receding hairline for this reason.

The kapha woman

If a vāta woman wants to make the world exercise, and a pitta woman wants to manage the world, what about kapha?

A kapha woman wants to feed everyone. Loving, sentimental, with a tendency to gain weight, kapha women tend to garden, cook, and feed others. They are natural nurturers. They are also stubborn and hate to make a change. (I should know, I am one!)

Kapha is a combination of water and earth.

Governed by a combination of sattva and tamas (mode of goodness and mode of passion), their dominant qualities are heavy, slow/dull, cold, oily, liquid, smooth, dense, soft, static, sticky, cloudy, and gross.

Bodywise, kapha women are the heaviest of all three body types. They are also the most stable, most stubborn, and most stoic. It is hard for them to lose weight. They can overheat quickly and may feel heavy after eating.

Like vāta women, kaphas also have cold hands and feet and tend to feel cold. Their skin is smooth, bright, and soft.

They stroll compared to a vāta woman, have a slow way of talking, have slow digestion — you get the gist.

Kapha women will be attracted to nurturing professions that resonate with earth elements. Chefs, cooks, teachers, caretakers and healers are often kapha women, for example.

Kapha women are either doing some charitable work, or trying to feed or help someone. They are natural couch potatoes. A kapha may sit on a couch, binge Netflix and munch on snacks for hours without feeling any need to exercise. They also love to sleep, be lazy and get pampered.

Sexually, kapha women may not have the playful energy of vāta or mad passion of pitta, but they have sexual stamina that the other two constitutions cannot outmatch.

Dullness exhibits itself as a dull appetite, feeling dull pain instead of intense or slow and sluggish digestion.

The quality of stickiness means good and bad; everything sticks to them. Weight, pounds, are hard to get off. If someone said something to a kapha woman 20 years ago, it is held in the corner of the mind.

Hence, it is hard for them to make changes due to this sticky quality.

When imbalanced or during PMS, menstrual cycle mind feels cloudy.

The liquid quality of kapha results in edema, water retention, tender breasts, or increased vaginal secretions.

To give an example, if you are kapha, then qualities of cold and heavy will lead to weight gain, lethargy, allergies, colds, water retention, excessive sleep. The kapha quality of dullness will lead to insecurity, depression, laziness, and greed. We will therefore suggest activities to stay warm, eat cooked warm foods with some heating spices, and drink warm tea.

To balance doṣas, Āyurveda suggests

- Doṣa pacifying diet

- Herbs
- Daily routine
- Seasonal routine
- Meditation
- Seasonal detoxification
- Doṣa pacifying exercise
- Massage and bodywork with warm oils and herbs

We will talk about how to balance our doṣas in later chapters.

What is a disease in Āyurveda?

The western medical system reduces a disease down to a singular cause, for example, a disease caused by a virus, a disease caused by bacteria, a disease caused by toxins, a disease caused by an overactive thyroid, or caused by a side effect of a drug or caused by the growth of cell and so on. In comparison, Āyurveda looks at the complete picture.

The disease is much more than a physical imbalance from an Āyurvedic perspective. Practitioners will look at signs and symptoms in a much broader context. They may consider loneliness, a lack of social life, or lack of familial support to be a cause towards disease.

Other causes of imbalance include:

1. an unbalanced diet;
2. eating foods incompatible with the doṣa;
3. improper sleeping habits;
4. negative thinking;
5. eating at the wrong times;
6. not following the cycle of nature;
7. going against your doṣa;
8. and suppression of natural urges that include sleeping, eating, and evacuation.

In women, it also includes:

9. lack of rest during the heavy days of the menstrual period;
10. eating a diet that disrupts the balance of hormones;
11. not de-stressing;

and much, much more.

The keyword here is imbalance instead of disease. For each individual, the manifestations of signs and symptoms, and their condition is unique to their constitution. Āyurveda aims to find a person's customized doṣik balance. The idea is to balance the mind and body synergistically. However, each person has a different 'balance' point before they tip over. Kapha, pitta, and vāta all have various manifestations of imbalance in their body; however, some symptoms may be similar.

Āyurveda considers the human being as a whole. Their doṣa, genetic code, social circle, satisfaction at work, aspirations in life. Consideration is even given to a person's general life karma via their astrological chart.

Miseries, suffering, and karma

There are three types of miseries or sufferings. The message here is that there are internal miseries, miseries due to other beings, or simply miseries arising from the environment:

- Internal miseries
- External miseries
- Act of God or nature

Internal

These are miseries which arise from the mind and body such as disease, mental disturbance, emotional pain, grief, etc. Although all humans suffer these, they tend to disturb women a little bit more due to our genetic and mental makeup.

Other living beings

These are miseries caused by other living entities such as dog bite, snake bite or insect bite. Intestinal worms, the suffering caused by war, conflict and the envious or hateful actions of others is also included in this category of external miseries.

Act of nature

Suffering caused by seasons, environmental extremes and natural disasters, floods, tsunami, snow, extreme cold, extreme rains, extreme heat.

In addition to the miseries or sufferings defined above, we also have suffering stemming from karma. Let's explore this concept of karma a little bit more.

The karma

The word karma has woven its way into modern society and often has a negative connotation that there will be instant retribution. However, the karmic reaction can take years or even lifetimes to manifest.

Karmic reactions will affect children, parents, family. It is more complicated than "I parked in your parking spot, so someone else will park in mine." What our mother ate, thought, and did while she was pregnant with us affects us while we are still a fetus in the womb (mother's karma affects the baby after she is born).

There are certain prohibited activities during pregnancy which incur karma for the baby. I will talk about this later on in the book.

Let's first talk about Karmic reactions. There are generally two types of reactions.

One type of karma are reactions resulting from our own activities or those of our ancestors. This type of karmic result helps determine what kind of family we were born into our health, and our wealth. These are not under our control.

There are also karmic reactions we are due to receive but haven't actually received yet. This unpaid karmic debt that hasn't been assigned for collection can be reduced. It may also be removed via rituals and creating new, better karma. In reality, there is some sense of control in these karmic reactions.

Sometimes, women have a complicated relationship with their mothers and sisters. This may be due to karmic imbalance from the past. At other times, disease may manifest due to past-life activities.

Āyurveda not only wants to balance the doṣas and bring about mental equilibrium, but also suggests spiritual activities to help reduce our karmic debt.

When someone visits me for a consultation for the first time, my job is to determine who I am working with, who they are instead of what they are. My job is to focus on you as a WHOLE person. As an Āyurveda practitioner, I have to take into account your beliefs, values, diet, likes and dislikes, and last but not least, the life that you lead.

The life that we lead determines the karmic debt we receive in terms of suffering or happiness.

Four types of lifestyles

- Auspicious life
- Inauspicious life
- Somewhat happy life
- A miserable life

Āyurveda, being the art or science of life, focuses on four classifications of lives led.
Think of these as four categories of lives we chose to live, or lives we may have been given due to our past karma.

1) **Auspicious life** (hitāyus):
A life filled with consideration not just for others but also for mother

earth, a life guided by a moral compass, truthfulness, and living in harmony with nature.

An auspicious life is lived with a specific code, rules, and regulations that support us and our environment.

The aim and objective of Āyurveda is to live our best life. This best life can help us advance to a higher plane in our next life.

To help our physical, mental, and spiritual bodies, we must follow some rules and guidelines.

2) Inauspicious life (ahitāyus)
This kind of self-absorbed life is the exact opposite of what I said before. It is an inconsiderate life, a life not synchronized and in harmony with mother nature or other people. Living out of sync with our immediate environment is definitely inauspicious. It is a self-absorbed life, not living in harmony with nature, other entities, and the environment.

It is not good when we are self-absorbed, and our only focus is "I, me, mine," without regard for mother nature or other people around us. It leads to cumulative karma of bad results that can last more than one lifetime.

3**) Somewhat happy life** (sukhāyus)
Most of us fall under this category. In this category, a person may have a somewhat happy life, even though it may not be all auspicious.

When someone gives partial consideration to nature, nature also gives them partial consideration. When we sometimes do good deeds and at other times behave selfishly, we get a mixed bag.

Let's think of a mythical person called Jane Doe.

Jane Doe is mostly self-absorbed but will sometimes help her elder neighbors. Perhaps she recycles and is considerate of her sister's children, though she hates her sister.

Jane is very obsessed with making money, gossiping all the time, and keeping up with the Joneses. On the other hand, she recycles, is a partial vegetarian, is charitable around festivals, and sometimes volunteers at a soup kitchen just to post her "volunteer" selfies on Instagram.

Even if it's for selfies, charity and volunteering will still receive somewhat positive results. Such a person will get mixed results.

4) **A Miserable Life** (duḥkhāyus)
This category of life is terrible. Someone who lived an inauspicious life will get depressing karma in their next life. These results may include disturbed mental and physical state and a life full of misery. I call it the negative karma.

Negative karma is like a bank account in the negative. We have borrowed against the money we don't have. Now accumulate good karma and pay off that karmic debt. This is the state when we receive maximum physical, mental suffering.

Importance of digestion and elimination

Timely and balanced elimination is the key to wellness.

Āyurveda is based on the premise that we are not only what we eat but also what we digest. What goes in must come out — and on time. If it stays in longer, it causes trouble.

When kids come in for the first time with their parents in my office, they are greeted with a potty chart. It is amusing for children. However, the subject of excellent or poor elimination is often a very tricky one for grownups.

A chiropractor friend once told me that he muscle-tested a patient and found that constipation and irregular elimination increased their symptoms.

When his patients have regular bowel movements, their back pain seems diminished. Āyurveda believes if we are constipated, gassy, or have digestive imbalances, we will be imbalanced. Period.

We should make sure we have a healthy elimination.

"A potty a day keeps the doctor away" is the motto.

After all, Āyurveda believes that balanced elimination is KEY to good health.

Please refer to the chapter on Āyurvedic nutrition, where we talk about this in more detail.

Parīkṣā (assessment and energetic biofeedback)

The self-assessment questionnaire to determine natural profiles or doṣas is part of a test called parīkṣā. Āyurvedic practitioners may use many forms of parīkṣā - threefold, eightfold, or tenfold forms of parīkṣā.

The most common and most accessible that you can use for yourself is the self-observation and self-interview method.

It is a common misconception that we cannot evaluate ourselves. In fact, we are the best judge of our own spirit.

Women are naturally intuitive. We live in our own bodies, and we walk in our own shoes. No one else can walk in our shoes. Trust your gut and use these activities in the coming chapters to help you do a self-assessment.

In the following sections, I have created an activity on self-observation, questionnaires on observing and acknowledging your five kośas (layers), finding out your doṣa, your digestive assessment, and so on.

Āyurveda practitioners need the same input from you to make an informed decision before you go for a consultation.

When you consult with an Āyurvedic practitioner, they may use biofeedback from pulse (this energetic pulse is called nāḍī) at the base of the wrist.

They may check the state of the tongue. The tongue is the mirror image organ map, according to Āyurveda. They may check your marma points, which are sensitive areas in your body.

This will all be under the purview of a threefold check of observation, touch, and interviewing.

When a client comes to me, I need to understand the state of their doṣas, mind, body, and spirit. Using nāḍī, tongue inspection, an energetic scan, as well as interviewing techniques, I reach that conclusion.

I know you by what you tell me.

Once I determine the original constitution, the current imbalance, we talk about health issues and determine the causes of an imbalance. The idea is to remove these causative factors (hetus).

I end up educating most of my female clients about the healing benefits of a plant-based diet, unprocessed food, kitchen spices that are natural healers, and herbs for their psycho-physical constitution. (Suited to their temperament, body, and mind constitution at that particular time in their life!)

One of the reactions I get is amazement. "But that is so simple," some ladies tell me. Yes, Āyurveda is about incorporating simple changes, like drinking warm water in winter, and avoiding cold water, cold drinks. If that is not simple, and common sense – what is?

Why does Āyurveda resonate with so many women? Why is it one of the fastest-growing alternative health modalities, and so popular with women all over the world?

This is because Āyurveda is based on consciousness. I cannot stress the important role of consciousness, even though it is sometimes downplayed in Āyurveda articles on the Internet.

Fundamental Theories

Theory 1: Opposites attract

Opposites attract, right? Well, Āyurveda thinks so too: we choose opposing qualities to help balance us." Opposites attract. Right. Āyurveda believes that also. It is usually as simple as choosing the opposing attributes to help restore us.This is the theory of similar and dissimilar applied to protocols.

We help balance with opposite qualities.

For example, let's say you are a vāta woman with air and space element dominant. You can help balance yourself by the contrasting earth and water qualities that will ground you.

What are we grounding exactly? We are grounding the air and space elements. For example, choosing grounding earth foods like whole grains cooked with clarified butter will support the feeling of being spaced out.

Perhaps you get light periods, and the air and space elements manifest as anxiety and worries.

We can help balance that by the contrasting earth and water qualities that will ground your air and space elements. For example, choose grounding earth foods like whole grains cooked with ghee. (clarified butter).

Another good example would be cayenne pepper. A pitta person is dominant in the fire element. So, cayenne would NOT be suggested for a pitta woman.

Cayenne has inherent fire and heat qualities, and its energetics are harmful to a pitta person (similar attributes are harmful).

However, cooling coconut water (dissimilar attributes are beneficial) would help this pitta woman with fiery characteristics.

If you are a kapha woman, avoid earthy foods. What are earthy foods? Earth is wheat, milk, and most animal-based foods.

Kapha woman's earth element manifests as excess weight, so earth-based foods (like wheat or animal-based foods) and water-based foods (like milk or fruit juices) lead to imbalance. As an earth-dominant woman, you'd be better off with drying things like dried fruits, beans, or foods that increase heat and reduce water.

Theory 2: What is outside influences what's inside

According to this Āyurvedic theory, if it is happening outside, it is also happening inside. The premise is that everything that exists in the vast universe also appears in some form in our physical body. It's called the theory of microcosm and macrocosm. (We Āyurveda practitioners love to use bombastic words!)

In other words, you and I are mini versions of mother nature. We have a tiny miniature version of the universe inside us. We are a small miniature of the world.

To give you a simple example, the rays of the sun are microcosm or a minute particle of the sun. It has heat, light, and all the qualities that the sun has in a very minute amount. The universe has attributes that are all found in our own bodies.

We are made of the same essential elements that the world is composed of; isn't that amazing?

Just like all organic matter is made up of essential elements of carbon, hydrogen, and oxygen in chemistry, this theory is saying something similar. Our body and mind reflect what goes outside in the environment. We will talk about that in detail in the later chapters.

Āyurveda uses all of this to help balance us. We don't have to study and educate ourselves on all of this. Below are Āyurvedic considerations and suggestions that may aid in balancing our doṣas.

- Diet & nutrition to pacify our doṣas
- Daily regimen and seasonal regimen
- Exercise or yoga suited to our mind, body type
- Herbs and herbal formulations tailored to the imbalance, person, and doṣa

Chapter 2: Āyurveda and women

Women's natural roles

Let's talk about who we are as women. From where does our energy originate?

Our feminine body is a temple of nurturing and love. Our mind is our altar, and our soul has an intrinsic need to give and receive love. We are mothers, sisters, partners, wives, friends, and daughters. We are a minuscule version of mother nature and embody the role of Mother Divine. We have internal antennae, which are tuned to receiving the multitudes of energies around us.

We collect all kinds of energy from our internal antennae.

We are programmed by Mother Nature to care for others. We have the paramount ability to sustain life in our wombs and bring forth that life into this world. We are natural caregivers.

The women who choose not to, or who are unable to become mothers biologically, still have an inherent instinct of caregiving.

Such women may sometimes naturally choose nurturing professions or pour their maternal instinct into their family, work, or community. My son has a teacher who doesn't have any children of her own. She dotes on her students and cares for them as if they were her own.

I had a neighbor without children or siblings. She poured her love into her animals and pets. It's the same story; a natural nurturing and caring instinct manifesting in another form.

According to Āyurveda, women are uniquely governed by the energetics of the lunar cycle or moon cycle.

This connection to the moon increases gentle or softer energy in women, causing women to be ruled by emotions rather than logic.

This energy even has a name: soma. This energy affects the onset of a woman's menstrual cycle and typically coincides with the presence of a new moon.

While growing up in India in the '70s and '80s, I saw women occupy professional roles such as teachers, nurses, doctors, caregivers. I was told by my teachers, mothers, and aunts that these professions were gentler and suitable for ladies. I would argue in favor of women being able to do anything and everything.

However, as I have grown older, I have come to realize that women are naturally programmed by Mother Nature herself. Mother Nature is our presiding deity; she is not only our mother, but she is also the source of our maternal and nurturing energy.

We naturally embody these caregiving roles like doctors, healers, teachers, and nurses. However, we also dominate in other occupations such as musicians, scientists, engineers, architects, or singers; indeed, any purpose, depending on our doṣic affinity. Choosing a profession that is symbiotic with our dominant doṣa will work best, as this does not unnecessarily tax or stress our biological, emotional, or spiritual systems.

An imbalance may occur for specific doṣas like a sensitive vāta woman in active combat, or in competitive sports. Pitta-dominant women with Mars energy would handle such professions better. For some vāta women, certain occupations that require a lot of mental energy may give them more stress compared to a pitta woman.

Specific caregiving roles and occupations provide most women with an opportunity to embrace their innate inner nurturer.

Women in the workplace

After my time in the ashram, and my studies, I sought out employment in the corporate world.

While I worked in the corporate world, I continued to study my life long passion Āyurveda.

At this time, big American companies were creating call centers in Delhi and Gurgaon. I was hired as a communication and accent trainer. This was a throwback to my theater days, as I can imitate certain accents.

I was also asked to create an instructional design by some companies. This time working in a big American call center in India gave me time to study hundreds of people, especially women, in a stressful work environment in late-night shifts. Though my job was to listen to their calls and coach them on their accent and communication skills, my coaching ended up also being Āyurvedic. Sometimes I was giving out prāṇāyama, mantras, and suggesting herbs along with an official evaluation of their performance on calls.

I began to notice at this time that women were working during their menstruation. They would continue to juggle to meet the physical demands of their home and work. It is not easy to get out of bed, put on a business suit, commute to work, and meet deadlines while having menstrual cramps.

These physically taxing tasks were done instead of resting and soothing their menstrual discomforts. The accomplishment of all these physically and emotionally tiring activities is unnatural and only serves to deplete and exhaust us.

When I worked at the call center, I noticed that many women in their twenties were all showing menstrual disturbances, or had PMS and other imbalances. The graveyard shift and changes in circadian rhythms were creating havoc on their systems. I was also affected.

After I got pregnant, I quit and vowed never to do a graveyard shift ever again.

My husband often talks about the feminist movement in America post World War 2 and the bra-burning era. Women sometimes have to adapt to newer modern roles that naturally oppose their intrinsic nature.

To get back to my corporate stint, I experienced competition from both men and women in the working environment. However, despite the existence of working rivalry, there remained a robust supportive community between women.

In my personal opinion, some women in managerial positions dealt with projects and responded to people and situations in a *gentler, kinder, and more rounded approach.*

They did this by sometimes showing tough love, but with great outcomes. I also saw women trying to dress, behave, and talk like men to gain acceptance.

My prior life and work experiences have often left me to wonder, "Why have women transitioned into behaving and acting like men in numerous professions?" Women have a distinct role from men, and this distinction is often misinterpreted by society as inferiority. Women are not inferior to men; instead, the societal role played by women is so uniquely beautiful. At the same time, women are NOT superior to men either.

We are merely different and have a different role to play.

As women embrace their masculine side and suppress their femininity to compete with men, it can cause imbalances.

I have done thousands of consultations for women, and based on those consultations, I have concluded that suppression of our feminine side and feminine graces can lead to unhealthy habits, behaviors, and physical imbalances.

An example is one of my clients, who was in an unhealthy relationship where she was the prime earner. She worked, paid the bills, looked after the kids, and cooked.

She wore the pants in the relationship literally and figuratively.

She had her hair cropped, never had time to put on makeup, and always wore suitable unflattering clothes.

Part of my regimen to help her dosha and physical imbalances was to ask her to get her hair styled, wear a little makeup, flattering outfits, and pastel shades.

I wanted her to look in the mirror and admire herself for one minute every morning.

One of my students helping me with editing read this sentence and told me that this would upset people. I stand by my belief; suppressing femininity is not healthy. Accepting our feminine side means we are coming from a place of power.

In Ayurveda, the origin of the disease is due to HETU or the cause of the problem.

The underlying premise is that when we remove the cause, the imbalance will slowly disappear. Example: if a toxic relationship is taxing and gives mental stress, cutting ties will actually be healing. There are many causes of imbalances.
Three key causes of imbalances are:

Ignoring our inner voice
Overusing, Underusing or Misusing our Senses
Impact of Climate Change

CAUSE OF IMBALANCES

Case Study

Roe (name changed) was from a very conservative family. She had immigrated to a new country with her husband in search of a better job and future for herself.

She was lonely for her family back home, suffering from culture shock in a new place. It was hard for her to be at the top of her game in her employment.

She was finding it hard to concentrate and focus during her PMS and the first two days of her monthly period.

The natural release of menstrual fluid cleanses women physically, mentally, and emotionally. This is not a time to travel or do heavy mental or physical work. When I worked in the corporate world, I used to see quite a few women show up to work with the symptoms associated with the first day of their menstrual cycle - bleeding, bloating, diarrhea, or constipation. They were mentally spaced out, drugged up to their ears, and avoiding resting (remember, these were graveyard shifts).

I asked Roe if she can take a personal day off on the first day of her period.

She said that she only got two personal days a month that she had been saving up for her vacation. She really didn't want to give up her vacation days.

However, once she started doing this and used her personal day for some rest and relaxation, it actually helped her be more productive at her job.

She started using her days of periods for more mundane tasks and scheduling essential meetings online, or after her heavy days were done.

The inner voice

Remember the inner voice that stops us from doing something wrong. That inner voice is our *consciousness*.

All of us hear that inner voice, especially as children, when we are more pure-minded. As we grow up, sometimes that voice disappears in the mind chatter and our busy lives.

In Āyurveda, not listening to our inner voice is called prajñāparādha. Translated into English, it is an offense against our intellect or senses.

This inner voice is the real voice of our intelligence and consciousness. Ignoring it is considered offensive against the divine, who has given our consciousness the ability to "talk" to us.

Sometimes, it is the divine itself, who is instigating this inner voice to warn us, or answer a question we have been seeking an answer to.

In other words, Ignoring that inner voice in our head, which represents wisdom, is not good and can lead to problems.

Women throughout history

Throughout history, ancient civilizations have worshipped the sacred feminine and Goddesses. In the Vedas (5000 b.c.), women occupied the role of Mother Nature. Mother nature was called prakṛti. She was analogous with the goddess Parvati, or Śivānī, who is the consort of Śrī Śiva, the destroyer. Mother Earth herself is personified as a female goddess called Prithivī or Bhūdevī (similar to Greek Gaia). See Chapter 7 for more information on the goddess.

She is the consort of Śrī Viṣṇu's third incarnation, the divine boar Varāha, who acts as the protector.

The feminine half of the earth is the minuscule representation of the energetics of creation. This gives rise to a woman's ability to procreate. Procreation includes giving birth, but also includes being friends, wives, mothers, sisters, healers, and caregivers to all those who surround us. These uniquely beautiful qualities are why women have been celebrated, respected, and revered for thousands of years.

According to Āyurveda, there are three crucial phases in the life cycle of a woman. The first phase is called yuvatī, and it begins at the reproductive age or menarche. The second phase is referred to as prauḍhā (middle-aged) and occurs between forty to fifty years of age.

The third phase is called vṛddhā and begins approximately fifty years of age and continues until death. I will discuss in detail about these three cycles of a woman's life in the second chapter.

Phase 1	Child 0-13 years (bala)	Influenced by kapha
Phase 2	yuvatī (child-bearing age)	Influenced by pitta
Phase 3	prauḍhā (middle-aged)	Influenced by vāta and pitta
Phase 4	vṛddhā (post-menopausal)	Influenced by vāta

According to the Vedas, women are not identified with a physical body; instead, women are a spirit (ātmā) who resides in a physical body. Women are a spirit, a soul, and a piece of Divine energy. In the Bhagavad Gītā, it states that the spirit is very small (1/10,000 the size of the end of one single hair), and it resides in the heart.

The presence of a woman's spirit in her heart is why prāṇa (or Chi) lies in the center of the heart. From this core, prāṇa nourishes the entire physical body, mind, and consciousness with its pure energy or life force.

The Vedas, ancient literature written five thousand years ago, describe seven mothers called dhātrīs. Humanity was expected to respect all of them as mothers.

- *ātma-mātā*: Our biological mother
- *guru-patnī*: the wife of the Guru or master
- *brāhmaṇī*: the wife of a *brāhmaṇa* (a qualified priest)
- *rāja-patnikā*: the wife of the Leader or a King
- *dhenu*: the nursing cow
- *dhātrī*: the nursing mother (who may or may not be the same as a biological mother) or the adopted mother
- *pṛthvī*: Mother Earth

According to the Vedas, we are not this body but the embodiment of śakti - the feminine aspect or energy of the Divine. We are the representative of Mother Nature, or prakṛti – chosen to give life and heal.

On a personal level, it is fascinating that many of our womenfolk, including myself, naturally identify themselves with a caregiving identity, such as mother, wife, or healer. The Sanskrit word strī means woman. Women were given a lot of respect in the Indian tradition and are often spoken of as representative of two Goddesses (Lakṣmī and Sarasvatī) who embody wealth and knowledge, respectively. A woman (strī) is also viewed as an embodiment of agni (fire), the energy of transformation revered in the Vedas. From an Āyurvedic perspective, agni is seen as the ignition or igneous event, and its presence in women bestows them with their natural luster.

The yoni

The Sanskrit word for a women's uterus and vagina area is *yoni*.

Personally, I like it a lot better than calling it vagina, vejayjay or fanny (British slang), no disrespect to those who use it.

Those phrases do not give enough gravitas and importance to our womb.

It is even a little demeaning, in my opinion, though some young women tell me that using slang makes it easier for them to talk about their private parts openly.

Yoni is respectful; it is a place where life is formed.

The word yoni comes from the joining of the sound ni to the root yu, which means mix and separate. It is the group of organs in which the woman and child are united and then separated, namely the uterus. This remarkable difference is what makes us different from men.

Yoni is said to be like an inverted lotus. It can expand when there's a baby in the womb. It can shrink. It changes during a woman's monthly cycle.

It is essential we meditate on our Yoni, respect it, be aware of it, nourish it, and take herbs to tone and strengthen that area. We should look after our yoni whether or not we choose to become mothers. Even women who have had a hysterectomy and do not have a yoni, still have it energetically.

The menstrual cycle

The monthly cycle of the woman is called the moon cycle or ṛtu in Sanskrit. Ṛtu means season. Just as seasons come and go in a sequence, so does our menstrual period. Hence, our monthly period is denoted as a monthly season with 15 days pre-season, and 15 days post-season aligned with the cycle of waxing and waning Moon.

We talk about the menstrual cycle in detail in chapter 3.

The menopause

Menopause is not just the cessation of monthly period. It is the end of fertility. It is the end of a long cycle. It is also a new beginning. It is the beginning of a new period of internal and spiritual focus rather than focusing on children, family life, and working hard to make money. It is a period where, over the years, we also grow older and prepare for our last phase.

The interplay of hormones affects the menopause. Many women have symptoms like hot flashes, digestive upset, mood swings. Āyurveda sees menopause as an opportunity to gracefully step into your new body, new rule, and age gracefully and beautifully.

Menopause is also discussed in later chapters.

Our inner layers (kośas)

One can say, Āyurveda doesn't treat the disease, but the consciousness, mind, and physical balance of a person.

Instead of asking what is your health issue, Āyurveda asks questions such as, "Who are you?" "Where is your consciousness?" "Are you situated in your own personal balance?"

Are you a mother? Are you a wife? Are you a girlfriend or a daughter? Are you overweight? Are you defined by your profession? Are you defined by your nationality?

Are you slim? Do you consider yourself beautiful? Are you tall or short? Are you dark or fair? Are you defined by the color of your skin?

Think about it. All the questions above pertain to your physical body and its proportions, or the relationships this body has with other people around you.

Our weight, height, skin color, state of matrimony, or lack of it defines our physical state in this world. However, it doesn't answer the question of who we are inside. We are not this body.

We are a spirit who resides in this physical body. We are MORE than just our physique. We have many layers, unexplored. These layers are called kośas.

The kośas – our layers

According to scriptures, we are a complex embodiment of five layers. In other words, we are made of layers, and we are complicated.

We are all unique, as our layers are unique. We are a result of combination and permutation of our karma, our lifestyle, our activities, our dharma(duty), our thinking, our diet, and our environment, resulting in different complex layers in our identity.

Āyurveda and yoga practitioners call our layers the pañca-kośas (the five levels of our existence). We interact with our outer world via one or more of these layers at all times.

- The gross physical body (annamaya-kośa)
- The energetic level (prāṇamaya-kośa)
- The mind (manomaya-kośa)
- The intellect (vijñānamaya-kośa)
- Blissful consciousness (ānandamaya-kośa)

The outermost layer

Our physical level (annamaya-kośa)

Our physical body is our outermost layer. We also identify with this layer as "I" and "me."

I am thin. I am fat. I am hideous. I am gorgeous. I have acne. My skin is horrible. My skin glows.

However, we are not our physical layer. We LIVE inside it. If we are driving a car, you won't say, "I am the car." You will say, "I am the driver." Similarly, the physical body is our vehicle commandeered by our soul and intellect.

This kośa or layer is deeply defined by food and consumption. When women are happy with their annamaya-kośa, they will eat more mindfully. When we are unhappy, we may gorge and stuff ourselves with food. We may go for a long run, or clean the house. I bake and cook up a storm (then eat it).

This is because the focus of annamaya-kośa is gross nourishment, taste associated with gaining weight (fats, fried things, and sweets) and with simple emotions of security associated with infancy and toddler age.

Outermost Layer
Level of awareness: Physical body
Focus: Identifying the physical body
Problems: These are lack of discrimination, selfishness, tendency to overconsume, reinforcement of regressed emotional state; greatest tendency to lead towards obesity, diabetes, etc.

The energetic layer

The second layer is the layer of vitality.

Ever had a feeling when something makes you feel alive? This feeling of being alive manifests at this level. Trying to eat better, exercise, our sexual desires, all are felt at this level. When this kośa is imbalanced, we may be socially irresponsible in society. For example, during the COVID 19 situation early on, many young people in different countries totally ignored social distancing and went to work out or visit beaches. The imbalance is thinking, "I am going to live forever; I am beautiful, young, and sexy." Being obsessed with exercise and the physical body would also be a part of this. Social responsibility, good citizenship, or voting is "not my problem."

The other end of the spectrum is not caring about our bodies at all and not exercising at all. This layer is called prāṇamaya-kośa because prāṇa circulates in this layer.

> **Second Layer**
> **Level of awareness:** vitality, energy, strength
> **Focus:** good health, vitality, energy, endurance, physical stamina, sexual ability
> **Problems:** lack of sensitivity, lack of awareness of impact (social and karmic)

The mind (manomaya-kośa)

The mind is the center of all activity, all perception. We live through our thoughts. It can be our friend, or it can be our enemy. This layer that encompasses us is the mind layer or manomaya-kośa. The mind is not the brain, even though the brain is a tool that the mind uses. Consciousness is not the nervous system though it indeed uses it as a tool. Mind regulates the five senses and all other working senses.

We can all eat a sweet mango or a banana but taste it differently. Perception of taste happens in mind. The perception of pain also happens in mind. The purpose of yoga practice is to calm the mind. You read earlier in my sixfold steps — put mind first before the body. If the mind is happy, the body will usually follow.

The Third Layer

Level of awareness: feelings, varied taste, complex emotions
Focus: an experience of varieties of taste, new and different experiences, some awareness and sensitivity
Problems: an obsession with taste reinforces bodily connection and may degrade into overconsumption and associated problems; the impetus for ever-fresh tastes may create stress

The fourth layer (vijñānamaya-kośa)

The intellect is the fourth layer that hides under the mind.

This layer is the residence of intellect. It can reason with the mind. When children start reading, they discover this layer. It is called vijñānamaya-kośa.

The Fourth Layer

Level of awareness: intellect based on facts, reason, and logic
Focus: eating for the benefit of self and others, awareness of the impact on the planet, awareness of the karmic impact
Problems: an obsession with avoiding impact may lead to extreme life choices, and may be challenging to integrate with modern life – not a problem per se but a potential issue

The blissful layer (ānandamaya-kośa)

The fifth and final layer, hidden like a gem in a treasure hunt, is the layer of bliss. This is where our consciousness resides.

If we think of all the kośas or layers that surround our soul as layers of an onion, the last part is ānandamaya-kośa. It's not a terribly great example, but the onion has layers. We keep on peeling the layers, again and again. We then get into the innermost layer.

This level or kośa lives within our spirit or soul. It gives us bliss. Bliss is different from happiness. Bliss is a state of awareness, a condition felt in body, mind, and soul.

Happiness is one emotion that is often felt in relation to our physical senses. A cupcake made you happy for a few seconds.

Bliss lasts longer than happiness, which is fleeting.

This layer is called ānandamaya-kośa.

> **Level of awareness:** spiritual connection and realization of ultimate bliss (not sectarian religious ideas)
> **Focus:** cooking, eating and sharing as an act of sacrifice, love, and connection with the greater spiritual whole
> **Problems:** problems reconciling with the modern workaday world and relatives

Case study -The inner voice

I had a client come in one day who had not slept properly in four weeks. She was underweight, had dry hair, dry skin, and tended towards constipation. She had cold extremities. Her monthly cycle was light. All the qualities of vāta could be seen in her signs and symptoms. She had mostly presented and wanted support with digestive issues, along with some support for anxiety, stress, and insomnia. Her original constitution was vāta dominant. Her current imbalance was also vāta.

Let's call her Anamika (Anamika means anonymous in Hindi). Anamika was looking for natural alternatives. We talked about her home, her goals, her diet, her lifestyle - the works.

I suggested the usual support guidelines for insomnia: no television at night, following a nightly ritual, and golden milk with nutmeg. I suggested meditation and Āyurveda tips and some Āyurvedic herbs like Brahmi, Ashwagandha, and so on.

As we were winding up during the last 10 minutes of our consultation, she told me she positively hated her job. Her face changed and became contorted with pain for a second when she said the word "work." I became concerned and asked her more questions. Apparently, the work environment was stressful, and she was passed over for promotion. Her boss and others bullied her in a passive-aggressive way. Nothing was said openly. My impression was that the tension from the bullying and their attitude had her on pins and needles. She said she couldn't sleep, couldn't eat, couldn't think and was simply miserable.

She said to me, "If only I could leave my job, I would just sleep better, eat better and be more healthy." Her inner voice had already told her what she needed to do, and she simply voiced it to me. She had heard her inner voice, observed it, even acknowledged it, and now she had expressed it to me. She just hadn't done anything about it yet.

I asked her if she wanted to meditate on her inner voice and also seek a therapist or a psychologist. I asked her to create an intention and meditate on it.

Anyway, her time was up soon, and she left.

Two months later, when she arrived at my office, she was a completely different person. She was glowing. She was sleeping better, eating better, and Āyurveda was working wonderfully for her.

She said she quit her job and found a new one really quickly. She was now in a much better environment, happier, and was not under constant stress.

She had listened to her inner voice and made changes. I never had to say anything. Without her listening to her inner voice, any Āyurveda, Vastu, or meditation I could have given her may not have had the same impact.

One of my students heard me talk about her inner voice. She quit her current job and applied for a new one. Weeks later, she told me that her inner voice was telling her to stop, but she wouldn't. When I talked about the work environment being a cause of so much stress, that it can lead to disease - something clicked in her.

Remember the six steps at the beginning of this book. Here they are again:

1. **Become the observer**
2. **Acknowledge what you observe**
3. **Create intent**
4. **Cultivate new habits**
5. **Work on the mind (body follows)**
6. **Surrender**

It's time for our first activity.

The activity on the next page is *Step 1- become the observer.*

Get a piece of paper — or better yet, use a journal. This activity is awareness for one week.

Every day take time out to observe and finish this activity. At the end of the week, you may see that your observation has changed.

There are columns for each of the layers or kośas we talked about earlier. Meditate on each level, starting from physical body to your fifth innermost layer for 30 seconds, and write what you observed internally.

Activity #1

STEP 1: Become the observer.

Our first rule of self-help is to observe our inner selves. We do this by closing our eyes and observing our inner layers. For the next few days, become the OBSERVER rather than the doer. Watch yourself without judging. Be aware of your thoughts and actions. Do this kośa scan activity every day consecutively for 3, 5, or 7 days.

Observe, recognize, and acknowledge your blessings and understand who you are. "I am not this physical body, I am much more, and I have a spiritual duty to my ātmā (soul). Through the various kośas, I need to nurture my body, mind, and ātmā. They are one package." We will use self observation and doṣa test forms to observe and recognize. The acknowledge portion partly comes from within you - we are just facilitating the process.

I teach this to my students before a marma or nāḍī class as a self-scan or self-observation.

What activities do I indulge in related to this kośa of the corporeal platform? Write down what you tend to do, or what you think you want to do. Examples: clean home, go for a walk, workout, or do nothing.

Physical layer (annamaya-kośa)	Scan your body physically from the top of your head down to your feet. Sparśa (Feel body temperature, areas of stiffness or pain, etc.) Gently feel your wrists, heart center, and face. Feel body temperature, roughness, or smoothness of the skin. Touch any areas of stiffness or pain. Write your observations in a journal. If you can locate your marmas, meditate on them.
Vitality layer (prāṇamaya-kośa)	Scan your aura or chi by imagining a layer around you. You can also visualize this is a bubble of light coming from inside you and spilling out.
Mental layer (manomaya-kośa)	Close your eyes and do a mental scan and observe any feelings from a third-person perspective. Write it down. (See chapter on creating an intention) Observe the inner voice emanating from your mind. Is it saying something? Did it say something that you did not hear before? If you do hear something, make a mental note of it - don't judge or think. Just observe.
Spiritual layer	Put your hands on your heart center, crossed one over the other. Or put your palms together in a praying position. Visualize that your soul and spiritual body lives here. Visualize a divine presence and your consciousness here. Say hello to your soul and consciousness. Observe any feelings or sensations. Write it down. (See chapter on nurturing our intentions.)
Bliss layer	What activities do I indulge in related to this platform? Write down what you tend to do, or what you think you want to do.

NOTE: It may take a few days of doing this before you become comfortable observing yourself and hearing your inner voice. Keep a journal and devote 3, 5, or 7 minutes to this activity at a quiet time consecutively for three, five, or seven days. Do this activity on any day except Saturday.

Activity # 2: ACKNOWLEDGE WHAT YOU OBSERVE

STEP 2: Acknowledge what you observe

Use this guideline to write what you observed in the last few days when you stepped into the shoes of being the observer instead of the doer.

Spiritual Acknowledgement

Using what you have observed from your inner voice, write down and acknowledge your blessings, mistakes, and your failings as well as your strengths. Even if you can't think of it, meditate on it. Use your unique journal to write this. Do this activity a few days after doing Activity 1. Give yourself time to think and digest what you are observing about your inner self first.

My inner voice says...........

My blessings include ....

The mistakes that I would like to rectify are...........

My strengths are ....

My failings made me stronger. For example ....

ACTIVITY# 3: The Doṣa Test

Fill the questionnaires at the end of the book before you move forward to the next chapter.

Questionnaire (use the questionnaire at the end of the book)

Determine your original and current constitution by finishing all three questionnaires at the end of the book. We have created two columns in these forms where you answer the same question twice. These are the natural and current states of your doṣa. Let's determine the original and current constitution and write down below.

a. Our original constitution or original doṣa lies between the time of birth to about age 13. This is your baseline. We call it prakṛti. This was predominant in you during childhood: what your tastes were, how you behaved, your appetite, your ability to memorize, your IQ, your EQ, how you dealt with onset of puberty, emotional and physical challenges, etc.

My original constitution (doṣa) is...

b. Now, we go through the same set of questions, emotional and physical challenges, food, diet, elimination – in the last few years. This helps us determine what has changed over the years. We are now determining the current constitution. Our current constitution is called vikṛti.

You can take the doṣa test at the end of the book to find out your current and original constitution and fill in the blanks.

My current constitution is……………………………………………...

Activity # 4

STEP 3: Create intent

Before we can create a plan or an intent, whether it is to make behavior changes, or bring more balancing or healing into our lives, we need to know our original and current doṣa.

Using notes from Activity 1, Activity 2 and Activity 3, create a PLAN, an INTENT of what changes you would like to see.

Your intent is YOUR plan-write it the way you want it. Color it, sing it -make it into a poem. The intent should not be HOW I will do it. It is how YOU will manifest it.

Remember those January wellness resolutions we take that only last a month. The intention is like a resolution, except you are WRITING it and praying over it.

You are offering it and asking for a higher power to help you attain your intention. It's a resolution that you are asking for help with. Use words like "I would like the universe to help me with......," "I envision....," "I aspire," etc.

The intent should have positive words and phrases. It should have a timeline and have week by week changes

MY PLAN:

Week 1
Week 2
Week 3
Week 4

Cheat days

Chapter 3: Women are creatures of cycles

Have you ever heard anyone say, Father Nature? It is always Mother Nature. It is an undisputed fact that across cultures, religions, and centuries, earth has been revered like a mother. Earth also has a cycle. She is the Yin of Yang, a manifestation of divine energy that sustains us. Her gravitational force, her bounty, and her body sustain all living beings. She is our energetic MOTHER! We are her daughters energetically.

What is the behavior of this non-biological "mother" of ours? She does everything in a cycle.

Everything rotates and repeats and comes back cyclically. Rotation of earth around her axis or the sun causes cycles of day and night as well as the seasons.

Earth's cycles cause cycles within the entities that reside in her "body" of land, air, and water. Trees shed leaves and become dormant in the winter as they wait for spring. Fragrant buds and flowers burst forth out of her in the spring. There is also a cycle for harvesting plants and food.

This feminine energy of the earth sustains and influences us at every possible level. We are part and parcel of this mother nature. Being part of this earthly planet, we also have a cycle. (This cycle portion also applies to men, however, cycles in men are less pronounced. For example, andropause in men over 50 happens slowly compared to the super-fast hormone roller coaster that women go through).

Every culture and every religion, most ancient societies lived their lives in sync with the cycles of mother nature. In fact, this term defines Āyurveda.

Āyur in Āyurveda denotes the “life we live.” Our objective should be to live a life of auspiciousness. This happens when we synchronize with mother nature.

Following the circadian rhythms created by the solar cycle and moon cycle and following a seasonal regimen is an integral part of this synchronicity.

It is essential to recognize that we daughters of mother earth are creatures of the cycle. If she is happy, we are happy. If she is unhappy, we are unhappy. Why do you think we women are obsessed with flowers, gardens, colors, and beauty?

Since we are talking about cycles, let's also touch on the cycle of life and death. We are born, we do our dharma and live our lives laid out from the blueprint of karma.

We grow old, and we pass on. Then, we are reborn in a new body.

Whatever takes birth in mother nature decomposes and returns in another form. Similarly, we also die, and then we return to a different body according to our karma. This is the cycle of life-birth-death-life again.

All of humanity is influenced and dependent on the cycle of sun and moon.

However, we women are a little more affected than most during waxing and waning of moon and seasons. These cycles cause an emotional, spiritual, and physiological change in our body and the five kośas. (The physical and energetic coverings)

The elements of air, space, fire, water, and earth are constantly reacting to change in our physical environment and earth cycles. This creates internal cycles within us to sync with mother nature.

The cycle of the sun

Girls up to 12 years of age and up are called bālikās. This means a girl who has not yet had her period. At the age of 12 or so, whenever the girl gets her first period, this is called menarche.

There is a ceremony called upanayana-saṁskāra, almost like a Vedic version of Bar Mitzvah for 12-year-old boys. In ancient times, this was done for both girls and boys. This is a time when the 12-year-old receives three sacred threads, mantras, and is given blessings to face the teenage years and his or her advent into adulthood. In India, women after the dark ages were denied gāyatrī or dīkṣā mantras. This practice in our monastery was introduced by Śrīla Bhaktisiddhānta Sarasvatī Ṭhākura in the early 1900s.

Vedic culture calls this ceremony upanayana-saṁskāra. It is the invocation for the three goddesses and the gāyatrī mantra, which itself is an invocation to the goddess. (As well as the supreme Śrī Viṣṇu, the male aspect of the Divine)

This time from 12 years of age, throughout the teenage years and even up to 45 years of age, is ruled by the sun (pitta). There is transformation, and so many life events happen here in life. This is also the pitta stage of life in both male and female genders.

- ***Menstruation:*** Monthly cycle or monthly period
- ***Menarche:*** The very first period in the life of women (at age 12 or 13)
- ***Premenopausal:*** From 10 yrs before through menopause
- ***Menopause:*** Complete cessation of the menstrual cycle
- ***Postmenopausal:*** 1 year after the menopause

Returning to our original thought, we have understood that we are cyclic creatures.

We start off in childhood blissfully unaware of what's going to hit us as a tween. This tween pre-puberty can be a confusing time.

This time includes the development of the breasts, the arrival of body odor, and eventually, the first period called menarche. As mothers, we should celebrate this time in the life of our daughters, and not make them feel ashamed or judged. Even that emerging body odor in a tween is the cause of celebration.

She is beginning to step into a time where she will enter as a child and emerge on the other side, a woman. It is a rite of passage. As a mother of two sons, I have only been able to enjoy this passage in my nieces and relatives' daughters.

When my son shaved for the first time, we took pictures and celebrated. He was embarrassed. I wanted to celebrate his rite of passage. I even made a whole celebration about acne facewash (He loved the Āyurvedic turmeric one best, yes!) and natural body deodorants.

Coming back to girls, daughters, and sisters – I want you to think about this. One day we were an innocent child. Suddenly we had our first period, and it comes every month, year after year till we are old. Oh no! This information can be so distressing for your little girl.

Explain to her that the beginning of menstruation is a rite of passage for a girl entering womanhood. Similarly, tell her about pregnancy being another rite of passage, and menopause being the last rite of passage, from a period of youth to middle and older age.

Other cycles include the birth of a child, the slow cessation of the monthly cycle (perimenopause), and finally, the complete cessation of menses (menopause) for 12 months and more.

The cycle of the moon

This is a more critical cycle for women compared to men. If I had to create a sequence for men, I would say the solar cycle probably affects them more than anything. However, for ladies, it is the lunar cycle.

This cycle begins to start around 45-50 years of age. In Āyurveda, it is referred to as vṛddhā. Growing up, I hated it that women over 40 were called vṛddhā. I have come to understand it doesn't mean that they are over the hill. It merely means that childbearing years are limited or finished.

As women, we are greatly influenced by the moon cycle.

In India, most of us tend to follow what we call a lunar calendar instead of the Gregorian calendar that is ruled by the sun and 365 days. The lunar calendar has two aspects- waxing and waning of the moon.

Mother nature has given us 28 days - 30 days during which we get our monthly cycle again. In fact, the build-up of estrogen and ovulation happens precisely in 15 days, and in the next 15 days are the build-up of progesterone -- and it ends up in the monthly bleeding.

The moon has a similar cycle. For fifteen days there is waxing and then the full moon. Then in the next 15 days there is waning and the new moon. Waxing in the moon cycle corresponds with the build-up of estrogen in our body. The moon affects our estrogen levels -- in an energetic way. Menstruating with a full moon is the best way to achieve balance.

The moon or Chandra is not ordinary. It yields power over us. It manifests and balances our feminine energy that presides over water, medicinal herbs, gives us the feminine charms, balances and delights our hormone levels, and is referred to as soma.

In scriptures, it is said that plants use light from the sun to create their food via photosynthesis, but the taste or rasa - the juicy sweetness of mango that melts in your mouth - manifests when it is exposed to the moon.

Moon gives rasa *(waters, taste, flavors)*

Moon controls the ebb and flow of the tides and life on earth. It has been found, for instance, that oysters will adjust their shell openings to when the moon is directly overhead.

The different phases of the moon affect the germination of seeds and the growth of plants. Bees are more active at new moon, and plant metabolism is at its highest at the time of a full moon.

The moon affects the menstrual cycle.

The energy of earth and air elements rules children. The period or menstrual cycle commences the pitta stage in a girl's lifecycle.

Case Study

During my first year of practice in California, I had this wonderful lady come in with some menstrual issues. Let's call her Joy because she had a lovely personality. Joy hadn't had a period for ten months after going off her birth control pills. She had been on birth control pills for nine years. She was not pregnant, and there was nothing medically wrong with her. Her schedule was erratic, and she ate, slept at different times every day.

I suggested lifestyle, daily routine, seasonal routine guidelines. She had to wake up, relax, and eat at the same time every day. I asked her to maintain a strict routine. We talked about a diet rich in phytoestrogens, and about doṣa pacification. We talked about some yoga poses that stimulate yoni and direct energy downward (Garland pose, squatting, etc.)

I asked her to avoid alcohol and caffeine. I suggested herbs like Shatavari, Ashwagandha, Licorice, etc. along with golden milk. (hot milk boiled with turmeric, saffron and flavored with cardamom)

I explained to her that women are creatures of cycles. If a woman takes a birth control pill for so many years, the body forgets to have a menstrual period. From the Āyurvedic perspective, we had to remind her of this cycle. Hence the strict daily, nightly routine was suggested.

In one month, she had a light period. In three months, her periods became normal.

The herbs, yoga, and a doṣa pacifying diet had supported her imbalances.

Case Study

I had a client once whose husband had passed away a year ago. She was a little lost. A friend of hers brought her to me for a consultation. We talked about Āyurveda, Āyurvedic diet, and so on. (Which did help her with her issues). I want to talk about her emotional state due to the tragedy.

I noticed she did not have any taste, any rasa, for doing anything other than the mundane. When people are down, they don't have that inner joy. I noticed her face had no makeup, her hair was unruly, and she was wearing all black a year after her husband passed. She was wearing these loose unfeminine clothes.

She had no path in life and was going through the motions. She was not depressed, mind you. She had a fulfilling job, friends, and children who loved her.

I asked her to create an intention of finding her path now that her husband was gone.

Besides, I had her put some clean water in a glass jar on a full moon and offer it to the deity of Moon and Mother Nature. She started going out on "full moon" walks. I suggested herbs like rose jam, tulsi tea, and massaging the heart point (a marma smack at the center of the palm) with essential oils of sandalwood and rose. She also agreed to get her pearls out as they are connected to the moon. I asked her to wear happier and lighter colors like yellow, pastels, etc.

I asked her if she was open to getting a makeover. She agreed. She got a beautiful haircut, got her charming feminine outfits and her pearls out of the closet, and started wearing white, cream, light, or pastel shades of clothes.

She finally found peace in teaching gardening, doing some art, and cooking.

She had found her rasa again. It took her a good six months to nurture her intention.

Āyurveda and the menstrual cycle

In Āyurveda, seasons are called ṛtu. The monthly cycle of a woman is also called ṛtu; it repeats like a season or a cycle every month. The menstrual cycle cleanses the woman's body of physical impurities like metabolic wastes, āma, unfertilized egg, uterine tissues, kapha impurities (mucous lining) of the yoni.

This is also a time of natural cleansing of mental fog, energetic blocks, etc.

The menstrual cycle is considered ideal when ovulation happens near the full moon, and menstruation happens around the new moon.

Even the cycles of ovulation, waxing, and waning have a relationship with the three doṣas.

Āyurveda has different names for the different times of the month of the menstrual cycle.

The woman who has a menstrual cycle now and is bleeding is ṛtumatī. It literally means "she is in season." The phrase used to drive me crazy during my feminist phase. I used to find it objectified and insulted womenfolk.

However, with age, I understand the layered meaning behind it. "I have my period. This is my season. Deal with it."

The Āyurveda texts mention that women can bleed either for 3, 5, or 7 days as the time period of a cycle. This would depend on her doṣa: vāta, pitta, or kapha.

When you take the doṣa test at the end of the book, you will see vāta, pitta, and kapha women have different manifestations, length, and symptoms of their moon cycle.

The vāta, pitta, and kapha women will exhibit a combination or permutation of one, two, or all three types of symptoms. This may be normal for them. A three-day cycle may be a vāta woman's baseline, or a 5-7 day cycle may be a pitta woman's baseline. These manifestations are listed below

Vāta	Pitta	Kapha
Duration: 3 days *Quantity*: Irregular and light bleeding Bloating Constipation Low backache Cramping Pain in pelvic area and legs Dry skin Dehydration	*Duration*: 7 days *Quantity*: excess blood flow Hot flashes Excess blood flow bright red in color Acne (heavy breakouts) Sharp cramping Headaches/migraines Diarrhea	*Duration*: 5 days *Quantity*: Heavy in the first two or three days, then light Feeling sentimental and lazy Heaviness in breasts Slow metabolism Wanting to cry Dull skin. May have breakouts.

The first cycle I want to talk about is the cycle of the menstruation. This monthly cycle is actually a cleansing ritual. It is ruled by moon, the lunar Deity.

Our monthly period is denoted as a monthly season with 15 days pre-season and 15 days post-season, aligned with the cycle of waxing and waning moon.

The phases have names like "pre-season" or "post-season" called ṛtukāla. Translated, it means preparing for the monthly cycle.

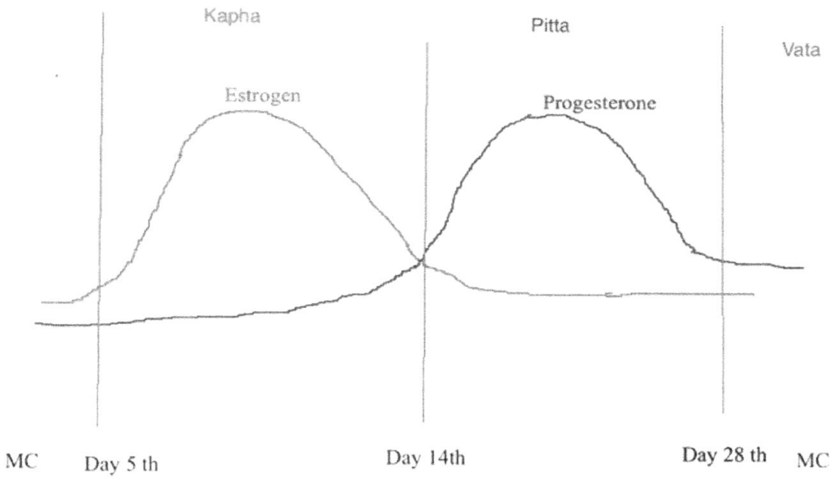

FIGURE 1: DRAWING BY DR. KIRTI PINGLE

Menses lasts (4-5 days) - With moderate flow, no clots, no discomfort.

Kapha Phase: The first 15 days after a woman's previous cycle is considered a kapha or buildup phase. Kapha influences the proliferative phase: This is the proliferative build-up phase after the period when the uterine lining is getting built-up. It is a kapha phase and is the best time for conception as ovulation happens in this phase. Estrogen is both a kapha and a pitta hormone.

Vāta Phase: The vāta phase helps in excretion of menstrual fluid. During vāta phase, fertilization does not take place and the uterine lining sloughs off. This doṣa is active in PMS.

Pitta Phase: Day 14 - Day 28 is the pitta phase. From ovulation to start of menses, progesterone is high. Ovulation to PMS is influenced by pitta energy.

When there is an imbalance in a woman's cycle, it is usually due to stress, poor nutrition, mental or physical imbalance, or hormonal imbalance.

Āyurvedically the downward movement force called apāṇa-vāta is usually involved. There is a famous yoga pose called apāṇāsana. It means a wind relieving pose. By bringing the knees to the stomach and pressing them, it directs the flow of wind downwards. This downward wind is apāṇa.

For example, a balanced apāṇa directs the downward flow of the blood.

A good menstrual cycle has the following signs:

1. Brightly colored blood
2. No clots
3. No slimy excess discharges
4. Bleeding is neither excessive nor less compared to the woman's baseline. (V, P or K women have different baselines).
5. Pain is mild and only associated during the cycle, not before.

When apāṇa is imbalanced, it can lead to painful periods, when in excess it can cause heavy bleeding, and when blocked, it may lead to blockage like PCOS.

1. Do not do heavy exercise when menstruating
2. Try to clean the perineum area every time you change a pad or a tampon
3. Wear organic cotton tampons or pad if possible
4. Use organic rose water/lavender water spray after using the bathroom
5. Use vaginal douches after the menstrual cycle is done

Practical Tips around Menstruation

Case Study

I had a client who had not had her monthly cycle after going off birth control for six months. She was very, very skeptical; I had suggested yoga poses, breathing, changing her lifestyle, and taking some herbs. How was this "voodoo" nonsense going to help her period back, she asked me.

I told her to trust the teachings for three months, and, if it didn't work, then she could simply stop seeking Āyurveda.

She was put on oil massages, especially belly massages, yoga, herbs like Shatavari and fenugreek, rose and other essential oils, and gentle yoga three times a week.

Four weeks later, she had one day of spotting. Eight weeks later, she got her period.

Case Study

An ex-student of mine, Mia (name changed), was on birth control for 6 or 7 years. She eventually got married, and soon they wanted to have kids.

When Mia got off the pills, soon thereafter, she was diagnosed with PCOS (Polycystic ovarian syndrome). Her monthly cycle, which was heavy and regular before she was on the pill, became light and irregular.

This is around the time she started using some alternative and holistic medicine practices. Using Āyurveda and other practices, it took her a year to get to the point where her monthly cycle was almost regular.

They had been trying to conceive for some years. She told me she wanted to have a baby who would be special and help the collective consciousness of so many people around him. I asked her to create an intention and pray over it.

She also agreed to fast from grains, lentils, and any animal-based food, and pray on a special day called Ekādaśī. (11th day of the moon, four days before the full moon or no moon).

She strictly fasted along with her husband. They also went to church and had someone pray over them thrice.

Within two months, she was pregnant.

She said she literally saw the light enter her, and she knew even before she took the pregnancy test.

Pre-menstrual syndrome (PMS)

Modern medicine has no explanation for this phenomenon except that it is related to the fall in the levels of Estrogen and Progesterone just before menses starts. From an Āyurvedic perspective, if a woman is balanced and healthy, her PMS would be mild. If she is unbalanced, then the PMS may have aggravated symptoms varied by the dosha.

Some of these include:

- Mood swings
- Irritability
- Bloating
- Weight gain
- Crying spells
- Anxiety
- Depression etc.
- Acne or breakouts

Vāta PMS	Pitta PMS	Kapha PMS
Physical manifestation Bloating, constipation, severe abdomen pain **Mental manifestation** Anxiety, restlessness **Menstrual manifestation** Scanty but very painful, irregular	**Physical manifestation** Hot flashes, adult acne, moderate pain in the abdomen **Mental manifestation** Anxiety, insomnia **Menstrual manifestation** Heavy bleeding, comes early, lasts longer	**Physical manifestation** Lethargy, tiredness, weight gain, dull pain in the abdomen **Mental manifestation** Crying bouts **Menstrual manifestation** Moderate bleeding but does not last long
Diet Warm vāta pacifying, warm water, grapes, dates, ghee **Herbs** Dashamula, Shatavari, Sesame seeds, Flax seeds	**Diet** Cooling & pitta pacifying, figs, melons, grapes, mangos **Herbs** Rose Jam, Shatavari, Ashoka, Pomegranate seeds	**Diet** Warm hot food, use of spices **Herbs** Ashoka, Kumari, Ashwagandha

Herbs and diet for menstruation

A lot of alternative medicine seeking women follow this plan called "seed cycle." I do love the idea; however, from the Āyurvedic perspective, it will be done with a twist. A seed cycle consists of taking estrogen rich seeds like Flax seeds, Chia Seeds, etc. in the first half of the cycle from day 1 of bleeding. From ovulation to the day before your periods begin, focus on estrogen- and progesterone-rich seeds like sesame, pumpkin, and sunflower seeds.

There are recipes out there. (delicious!) However, Āyurveda believes it is not good for all women. Kapha women who naturally make more estrogen in their body should take soy, flax, and chia in small amounts or avoid it altogether if imbalanced. However, vāta should take them in a lot more quantity. Pitta should take it in a moderate quantity.

Progesterone-rich seeds like pumpkin and sunflower should be favored by pitta and kapha women.

From an Āyurvedic perspective, the best seeds for vāta women are sesame seeds.

Other foods and spices for women include:

- Lotus seeds (tridoṣic)
- Rose (yes, eating dried rose jam) (tridoṣic)
- Fenugreek (vāta, kapha)
- Ajwain seeds (vāta, kapha)
- Shatavari (phytoestrogen)
- Walnuts (vāta, kapha in small amounts)
- Soy (for vāta only)
- Grassfed cow milk (vāta, pitta only)
- Ghee (vāta, pitta only)
- Sesame (vāta, pitta in minimal amounts)
- Sunflower (kapha and pitta)
- Pumpkin (cooked) All doṣas
- Pumpkin seeds - All doṣas in small amounts
- Turmeric
- Ashwagandha
- Punarnava
- Musta
- Vidari
- Sandalwood (pitta)
- The essential oil of rose (V, P, K)
- Dried pomegranate seeds
- Pomegranate molasses
- Pomegranate jelly
- Rose jam
- Rose syrup
- Rosewater
- Aloe vera

- Castor oil (for warm packs topically, and for massage)

Please see the chapter on HERBS and spices for detail.

Chapter 4: The menopause

Menopause is not just the cessation of monthly period. It is the end of fertility. It is the end of a long cycle. It is also a new beginning. It is the beginning of a new period of internal and spiritual focus rather than focusing on children, family life, and working hard to make money. It is a period where, over the years, we also grow older and prepare for our next phase.

The interplay of hormones affects the menopause. Many women have symptoms like hot flashes, digestive upset, mood swings. Āyurveda sees menopause as an opportunity to gracefully step into your new body, new rule, and age gracefully and beautifully.

When I came to the USA, I opened my first little office in San Diego. The focus of my practice was to give abhyaṅga (Āyurvedic massages). On my website, I also listed balancing Āyurvedic therapies for menopausal women. That and the abdomen massage on my website attracted a lot of perimenopausal, menopausal, and post-menopausal women.

Initially, it was to just get a massage or try something new.

However, many of them stayed on for an Āyurvedic consultation. Then they told their friend or sister, who referred to someone else.

Eventually, the word spread, and suddenly I had an entire practice focused more on women's support in Āyurveda than anything else. This happened organically.

Some hot flash pacifying protocols may include:

- Yoga, meditation before sleeping
- Use of jasmine, rose, sandalwood and lavender

- Head Massage - Cooling pitta oils, Kshirabala tailam, Women Support Oil from MAPI (self-massage at the crown of the head)
- Avipattikar Churnam, Amalaki
- Nasya with ghee
- For calcium and bone loss Pavala Pisthi (dried coral mix) supplement is suggested by Āyurveda. Ask your physician to suggest a natural calcium supplement.

Case study (menopause)

Noma (name changed) was going to celebrate her 50th birthday next year. Her relatives were flying down from all over. She was single, and her job and social life kept her very busy.

She initially came to me with her mother. Her mother had some persistent cough. I suggested some Āyurvedic protocols that helped the mom. Now, the mom set up an appointment for Noma to have an Āyurvedic massage with me.

Noma was shy and nurturing, a beautiful kapha woman. She had never had a massage, not once ever.

Apparently, she was having some shooting pains, some nerve issues, in her own words. She said her doctor had run all kinds of tests. There was nothing physically wrong. She was worried and anxious.

As I worked on her, I noticed her marmas associated with female imbalances were really sensitive. I asked her if she saw an OB-GYN for her perimenopause.

She said she is still having her periods like clockwork every 30 days. Her mother had a menstrual cycle until 54. She didn't even have any hot flashes, so she was not worried. I asked her to go anyway.

She called to let me know that she was indeed perimenopausal, and the therapy her physician started helped the nerve pain. Her mood was also better.

The moral of the story is that not all of us have hot flashes. Hot flashes are quite synonymous with menopause. A kapha woman might just have aches and pains and mood swings. If she does get a hot flash, she might dismiss it. She doesn't feel heat the way a fiery pitta woman does.

Case Study

I once had a student once who had a hysterectomy and was now in her late forties. In one of our class sessions, she asked about some of her symptoms. She had low energy, was irritated, sentimental, felt like she was burning up at night (though no fever), and suffered from insomnia. She had also changed in mood, and her private parts were dry. I told her she had some symptoms of menopause (there was nothing wrong with her medically).

She told me that she couldn't have menopause as she didn't have a yoni. I pointed out that physically her body may not have a yoni, but she is not just this body. She also has a subtle body inside her physical body. The subtle body still has all the limbs and organs energetically. Although there may be few or no physical symptoms, her body was still actively going through menopause. She decided to take some herbs like Chandana (sandalwood), Vidari, Brahmi (nervine support), and Shatavari (energy).

A month later, all her symptoms mostly disappeared. She was so blown away by the "energetic" menopause that she decided to help other women through this time.

Śakti

Below is an article I wrote for a journal. Even though it contains a lot of jargon, I think it explains in detail the respect and place womankind have enjoyed even in Hindu patriarchal society.

*The following article is a reproduction of an article written by me and published in a journal. (**Citation:** Groover MB (2017) Women Support in Āyurveda. J Tradit Med Clin Natur 6:e132.)*

Women have been celebrated as mothers in ancient texts, Hindu Upaniṣads and the Vedas, and given obeisances and revered for thousands of years. The Yin or woman symbol is part of the Taoist – yin / yang – where one without the other cannot exist. In Vedic tradition, all women and female mammals are part of śakti (The universal śakti - the Goddess - as opposed to the male śaktimān aspect of God).

Two important Sanskrit names for women are synonymous with their roles. One is ātma-mātā or the biological mother. The other word is dhātrī—one who nourishes a child. Dhā refers to the foundation, meaning one who gives foundation to a child whether as a biological mother, nurse, caretaker, or parent. The third more important synonym is śakti. Even though śakti is used for female goddesses, strī is given the special ability by Divine śakti to carry out her dharma.

For centuries, various ancient religions dating back to paleolithic times have worshipped śakti or goddesses, and the sacred feminine. Neo-pagans worshipped the Goddess as well as the Feminine.

Being a small part of the universal yin, the role of a woman is like that of Mother Nature. A woman is a minuscule embodiment of jīva-śakti (the Divine energy that manifests as innumerable souls). Strī is the minuscule energy of śakti, just like Mother Nature is a planetary manifestation of śakti energy on earth. The creative energy of Mother Nature works in cycles: cycles of seasons, governed by a cycle of the moon and sun, the progression of day and night, affecting the body, mind, prakṛti, and creating a temporary vikāra (vikṛti) at every junction for strī.

Hence, the fact that a woman is a minuscule version of this mother nature śakti deeply influences her body, mind, and spirit. A woman is affected by circadian and circumlunar rhythms, as well as by the junction of seasons. These cycles affect her times of menstruation and ovulation, and often coincide with the waves of hormones in a woman's body. These natural rhythms affect her more at different stages of life—whether a bala, yuvati, or vriddha (teenager, youth, or middle-aged).

The concept is that fertilization and reproduction are elemental dharma of a strī. Strī has the power to carry a life within her yoni. 'Yoni' comes from the joining of the word ni to the root yu, which means "to mix and separate." It is the set of organs in which the woman and child are united and then separated, namely the uterus.

Strī is an embodiment of agni. Agni is fire. This is a portrayal of the natural luster that women possess.

Interestingly enough, a women's constitution is predominantly made up of kapha doṣa. However, our reproductive systems are controlled by pitta doṣa, since blood and menstrual fluid is made up of pitta. For a man, their constitutions are predominately made up of the pitta doṣa, while their reproductive systems are controlled by the kapha doṣa. The physical difference between a man and a woman is only the extra srotās or channels of the women. There are 13 srotās (channels) in the male body, while the female body contains 15 srotās. Weirdly only our emotional differences, the way we are wired differently, is what separates us in society.

Although the woman is predominantly kapha, the reproductive aspect is pitta, since blood and menstrual fluid is pitta.

Direct cycles that affect the feminine energy are the macrocycles, moon cycle (menstruation), and the transitional cycles.

Macrocycle: The first change/cycle occurs at puberty when a young girl starts her monthly period. This is not just governed by the gravity of the moon, which also controls tides and even volcano eruptions but also the young girl's horoscope placement of her moon. Monthly up and down of Chandra (see explanation below), and waves of hormones control ovulation, monthly cycle, and pre-menstrual syndrome (PMS) that manifests differently in vāta, pitta and kapha women.

Moon cycle: As women, we are deeply affected by the Moon. The Moon controls our monthly periods, as well as our moods and minds. It does that in every person — however, for women, the influence of moon changes with its waxing and waning. I talk in detail about this below.

Transitional cycle – Childbirth: A woman's second transition is at childbirth. Āyurveda places importance on taking care of the woman at this transitional time as she reaches to fulfill her dharma. The younger the woman, the easier this transition.

Menopause: Five to ten years before the cessation of the monthly moon, the cycle is called perimenopause. In women, vāta energy will affect their body and mind at this time. Pitta energy will increase some years before and manifest itself in mood swings and hot flashes. After the cessation of the monthly cycle, vāta completely takes residence in the mind and bones. (Think how women are susceptible to osteoporosis at this time, and how vulnerable they feel).

Secondary cycles: **Seasonal Equinox, Spring, and Fall (Comes four times a year):** Ṛtusandhi, the junction of these seasons, affects the minds and bodies of women. This is not a time for women to start a new project. A journey, however, may be good for the restorative program or detoxification.

The moon and its importance for women

For this article, I want to focus on the connection of the menstrual cycle, and its connection to Chandra, the soma-cycle of Moon.

This is the MOST crucial cycle for women. If I had to create a sequence for men, I would say the solar cycle probably affects them more than anything. However, for ladies, it is the lunar cycle.

We women are ruled by the cycle of the moon.

Why moon? Moon is the giver of soma - feminine energy, taste and nectar to all plants. If not for the moon, the ṣaḍ-rasa (six tastes) won't manifest in the plants.

In India, most of us tend to follow what we call a lunar calendar instead of the Gregorian calendar that is ruled by the sun and 365 days. The lunar calendar has two aspects: waxing and waning of the moon.

Mother Nature has given us 28-30 days during which we get our monthly cycle again. In fact, the buildup of estrogen and ovulation happens precisely in 15 days, and in the next 15 days are the buildup of progesterone–and it ends up in the monthly bleeding. Moon has a similar cycle. Fifteen days there is build up and then the full moon. Then 15 days there is build down and new moon. Build up corresponds with a buildup of estrogen in our body. In fact, the moon affects our estrogen levels in an energetic way. Menstruating with a full moon is the best way to achieve balance.

Moon is not ordinary. It yields power over us. Moon presides over water and balances our feminine energy, increases the efficacy of medicinal plants, increases our femininity, balances and delights our hormone levels, and is referred to as soma. This sweet nectar of soma is called rasa.

In scriptures, it is said that plants use light from the sun to create their own food via photosynthesis, but the taste or rasa - the juicy sweetness of mango that melts in your mouth - manifests when it is exposed to the moon.

Why is this energy emanating from Moon so crucial to a woman? Moon influences all the waters in the earth, and all its plants, animals, and female creatures.

Moon is the controller of nectar and all water levels, and this is used by farmers practicing bio-dynamic farming. (Harvesting during Full moon)

The waters of the women are affected by the waxing and waning of the moon. These affected waters include menstruation and lactation. Moon also indirectly affects the hydration and plasma volume in our body along with bodily fluids, interstitial fluid, lymph, and the skin.

From an Āyurvedic Perspective, water element imbalance can be presented in two different ways:

- Increase of waters in the body leading to salivation, nausea, moist skin, and heavy menstrual flow.
- Decrease of waters leading to dryness.

Spiritually, moon gazing, moon yoga, and offering reverence to a goddess or Śiva-Pārvatī during Pūrṇimā (full moon) is suggested.

------------ End of the article ----------

Chapter 5: Pregnancy and post partum care

Āyurveda and pregnancy

A friend of mine who happens to be a physician was studying to be an Āyurveda practitioner in our school, while his wife was pregnant with their fourth child. After the birth of the baby, he wrote to me that they followed most of the guidelines for pregnancy in Āyurveda, and this was the best and easiest pregnancy so far.

If there is one place where Āyurvedic wisdom can help us, it is the journey of pregnancy. Instead of getting our information from apps on phones, tapping into this ancient wisdom can lay a foundation for a beautiful natural path during pregnancy and after. Āyurvedic guidelines provide month to month prenatal and antepartum rules for mind, body, spirit, and emotions. Āyurveda also firmly believes in the role of family and friends, social circle, and society during pregnancy.

The role of society, the country we live in, as well as our family is significant to the kind of pregnancy a woman will experience.

Family roles include help from family members and friends during pregnancy. In European countries or even Canada, a woman can take up to 9 months' leave after a baby is born. However, in the USA, only six weeks of unpaid leave may be given. This is an example of the role of society (or lack thereof).

In addition, fate also plays a hand. Fate is propelled by our karma. If we are to be blessed as mothers, no one can stop it. If it is not written, then it may not happen biologically or otherwise.

I once had a client who came to me for Āyurvedic massages. She had been put under forced paid leave after she almost died giving birth to twins in her forties. She said the most insightful thing to me. She said she was not supposed to have children due to some ovary problems. She used modern medicine and new technologies to get pregnant. According to her, almost dying during delivery and coming back was some sort of karmic payback.

There is a role of our past karma, our activities during the pregnancy that will influence the fetus. Similarly, we were influenced by our mothers when we were in their wombs.

Though most women in India will seek a medical doctor during pregnancy and birth, they are attracted to Āyurveda antepartum and postpartum as a supporting modality. This is also interwoven in Indian culture; these guidelines are passed from mothers and aunts to daughters.

For some strange karmic reasons, many mother-daughter relationships can be complicated. I tell my young mothers who come to me for spiritual consultations to put their problems and issues aside during the time of pregnancy. We need our sisters, friends, and mothers at this time. Holding on to anger, grudge, or hurt can be relegated to after the baby is born.

In the USA, women are choosing to have babies later than in any other decade. According to a survey published in 2018, 78% of women were childless between the ages of 20-24, and 54% were childless between 25 and 29. These numbers are different from the seventies, the eighties, or even nineties.

From a purely biological standpoint, the twenties are the golden years to have babies, as physically and energetically, we are in our most substantial period. This period of immunity and strength continues to decline as we move into our thirties and forties. I had a baby at 41, and it was so much worse than having one at 31 from all levels. I was breastfeeding two years later and having hot flashes at the same time. Not good!

Prasūti-tantra (Obstetrics) & Strī-roga (Gynecology) is the branch of Āyurveda that provides antenatal and postpartum care to women. We will talk about pregnancy month by month, the foods and list the guidelines.

I want to first start with conception, and the soul or spirit that is made to enter the woman by divine providence.

Conception and fertility

How can we talk about pregnancy and the postpartum period without talking about the actual act of conception?

When it's time for a new life to enter your body, no one can stop it. Providence will create the circumstances; cupid will create an atmosphere and desire.

And voila! Copulation will result in a new life in your womb. It is preordained.

Have you heard the saying we don't choose our parents, or we don't choose our children?

Well, I will let you in on a little secret. That's not entirely true from a Vedic perspective. Based on our past life karma, and our past life desires, providence shall choose parents that will give us the result of our previous karma. Yes, that previous karma from our previous life, a life that we don't even remember!

Āyurveda believes in reincarnation and past life karma and all that jazz.

Let me give you an example of a mythical person; let's call her JANE DOE. She lived in the 1800s in rural England. She was miserable, lived in poverty. But, she went to church and learned to be charitable in her previous life. She saw the injustices done to women and wished she could be a rich man.

Providence may make sure she returns in a new life as a boy in a wealthy family where her desires will come true, due to her charitable nature and good deeds. *(Yes, we can change genders and bodies in different births. That is a topic for another book.)*

You may be given birth in a noble family with money and charitable nature so you can continue to live out your Karma.

Now, if you were someone who went around cheating people in your previous life, you may be given the retribution of that karma in this life. *(FYI—we can do karma cleansing rituals and work our karma out in this life to receive better results. See chapter on meditation.)*

The bottom line is that a soul is sent under the direct supervision of the divine. How? It takes shelter of the seed or sperm.

When it's time for the soul to take a human body, the parents that have been chosen according to its karma will desire to copulate.

Alternatively, providence will make circumstances. Cupid may be asked to help the parents to be (if needed). Cupid is called Kāmadeva, the deity of love and desire in Vedic scriptures.

A soul is selected by providence, and its potential parents are selected based on its previous life karma. Then the circumstances are provided for mating. The soul is sent to the seed (sperm).

The seed retained in the yoni (uterus) already has a soul residing in it. It is the presence of the soul that gave the seed that extra zing to reach its destination and be the lucky one who got to mate with the egg.

If a soul has entered a woman's body, sometimes she may see a dream or a vision. I have had my lovely clients tell me that they "knew" when they got pregnant. Their doctor didn't believe them, but they claim they knew.

A client once told me that she had a vision of a baby boy with curly hair immediately after sex. She had a baby boy with curly hair. We women have this natural intuitive side that tells us what's going on. Unfortunately, our spidey senses get deactivated by spending too much time with electronic devices, running around and not listening to our own inner voice.

There are specific dreams that may be given, as well. A vision of baby on lotus may signify an auspicious pregnancy.

Before their child was conceived, one of my clients and her husband, followed some ancient Vedic rules for fertility quite strictly. They chanted and invoked higher powers for a qualified child. The grandparents also chanted and prayed. My client had a vision as soon as there was conception.

They were blessed with a profoundly gifted child with a genius IQ. (Yes, genetics probably had something to do with it as well)

I will give you my example, for my second born, I literally "heard" that I had been given a baby. I also heard sages chanting from the trees in Maui, in Hawaii.

During the day or different *tithis* of the moon, different souls may be sent down to our womb.

According to western embryology, the start of pregnancy is the day of implantation. From the Vedic perspective, the soul is already present before implantation, from the time of conception.

The reaction of sperm marrying the egg is not merely a chemical reaction. It happens due to providence providing a soul that seeks a home.

During the different aspects of the moon's waxing and waning, different souls may be sent down to the womb.

Pregnancy and Herbs

A rule of thumb is to avoid herbs and herbal supplements, especially in the first trimester. However, before delivery, herbs that are galactagogues are suggested in Āyurveda. These are fenugreek seeds, fenugreek leaves (methi), ajwain seeds, and licorice. Other spices include ginger for nausea; cardamom; cumin; coriander; and fennel for digestion.

After the baby is born, the mother needs to build her reproductive tissue and increase strength. While she continues to take her prenatal vitamins and added calcium, Āyurvedic practices suggest kapha foods, such as Shatavari with golden milk.

I just want to caution that most supplements and herbs are not safe to take during pregnancy.

A pregnant woman should speak to her health care provider before beginning to take any herbal supplements.

For instance, some herbs may cause uterine contractions, miscarriage, premature birth, and congenital disabilities.

Signs of conception

Signs that a woman has conceived include:

- salivation
- heaviness
- laziness
- goosebumps
- withholding of seed in yoni
- fatigue
- feeling thirsty
- the energetic activity of yoni (vagina; uterus)
- nausea
- stiffness in the chest area

Signs of pregnancy (garbha-lakṣaṇas)

Manifested signs when a woman is pregnant include:

- menstrual cycle stops
- salivation
- foods may cause nausea
- certain cravings
- nausea
- appetite changes
- eyes look softer
- breasts are tender / bigger
- dark areola of breasts
- feet may get swollen
- linea nigra (dark line on the abdomen)
- yoni dilates
- sensitivity to smells
- may develop allergies (which will pass after pregnancy)
- feeling sleepy and tired

Caring in the first trimester

A woman with a child is generally expected to eat smaller meals that are nourishing. She is eating for two, and her diet should be nutrient-dense, not calorie-dense.

A vāta pacifying diet with sweet fruits, well-cooked soft texture vegetables, comfort whole foods in small amounts spread over 4 or 5 small meals is suggested.

Favoring cooked foods to raw salads is essential.

In the first trimester, move to smaller meals, cooked plant-based diet, organic and sweet juicy fruits. Avoid produce that is conventionally grown, frozen, canned, tinned, deep-fried, or heavily processed. Avoid animal flesh.

A woman should favor all six tastes by focusing on juicy and sweet flavors.

First month

Symptoms:

- nausea
- breast tenderness
- fatigue
- frequent urination
- sensitivity to foods and smells

Diet: For the first month, the diet for a pregnant woman should focus on cooling, sweet foods, and fruits. Small quantities of meals should be given frequently. Golden milk with cooling herbs like cardamom, rose, and sandalwood should be taken, especially by pitta women (though this is suggested generally for all women, it is most beneficial for pitta). The milk may be sweetened with honey. Lots of soups and semi-solids are suggested.

Nausea:

- Ginger decoction for vāta and kapha women may support nausea.
- Cumin decoction (cumin boiled in water and cooled) may support pitta and vāta women.
- Fennel, cumin, ginger, and licorice with sugar candy may be helpful.
- Drink warm milk with cardamom or turmeric.

Ginger Decoction Recipe

A ginger decoction can be made by boiling one tablespoon of grated ginger in 2 cups water and reducing the 2 cups to 1 cup. Wait for it to cool and then sip it sparingly.

Cumin Decoction Recipe

Cumin decoction uses the same recipe; however, it is 1 tsp of cumin to 1 cup of water and reduced to 1/2 cup.

Tea with fennel, cumin, coriander may also help.

- Amla Candy
- Licorice sticks
- Cream (ice cream, if that helps)
- Ginger tea
- Lemon tea with honey.

Aromatherapy: rose, sandalwood, Khus (vetiver), lemon, orange essential oils

Second month

Follow everything from the first month.

Nausea may become severe — the same symptoms as the first month.

One Āyurvedic text (Aṣṭāṅga-Hṛdayam) makes this nice comparison. It equates the travel of sustenance between fetus and mother via the umbilical cord to an irrigation canal from a river to a farm that sustains plantlings.

Diet:

Juicy fruits, milk, and ghee should be part of the diet this month. The pregnant woman should continue taking sweet and cooling milk. If cows milk is hard to digest, goat milk or goat cheese is suggested.

She can also have cooling and hydrating liquids like coconut water, small amounts of vegetable and fruit juices (beets, carrots, oranges, ginger).

Herbs: In the west, Āyurveda practitioners do not suggest any herbs. However, in India, Shatavari, a uterine tonic, is commonly used. (Especially for a woman with a history of miscarriages). Other widely used herbs in India are Lotus root powder and Vetiver.

However, in the west, women are asked to avoid all kinds of supplements. Rightly so, because supplements and herbs can also be harmful.

Third month

Nausea may feel better for some.

Continue the diet and protocols from the first and second months.

According to Aṣṭāṅga-Hṛdayam, an ancient and crucial Āyurvedic text, the five parts of the fetus manifest in the third month - the head, two legs, and two arms.

The mother should prepare her mind as well as her body for the arrival of the baby.

She can do so by avoiding encounters that induce anxiety, stress, or fear.

Yoga and walking are the best exercises.

Avoid watching horror, sad, or scary television, for it can induce frightening energy onto the fetus. Avoid heavy-duty music like rock or heavy metal. Sweet classical music is best during this time.

The mother should be surrounded by a loving family. Besides, Āyurveda suggests that she should avoid traveling for long periods. This is not a time for athletics or extreme sports or weight lifting.

It is important not to get diarrhea nor become constipated during this time. Keeping an eye out on hydration, and fiber from vegetables and fruits becomes essential.

Last but not least, the mother should wear clean, light, loose clothing.

Diet: Same as month 2. If feeling indigestion, white rice gruel with ghee. Ideally, a bowl of rice called krishra is suggested. However, that is hard to find in the west, and a bowl of easily digestible rice like basmati is an excellent alternative.

Dairy: Goat's milk with honey.

Herbs: Same as month 2.

The second trimester

Finally, the expecting mother can see some relief from nausea and morning sickness. She will start to “show” this trimester. Keeping a daily routine — trying to wake up and sleep at the same time every day — is essential.

Topical massage with mild herbal oils is always relaxing.

With the nausea being over, a schedule of practicing meditation and mantras, daily walking, swimming, gentle prenatal yoga, and some breathing exercises can be incorporated into the weekly routine.

In Āyurveda, where the mother carries the fetus (front or back), as well as the shape of her abdomen, may indicate gender. *When the women is carrying the baby in the front, the old wives' tale says it may be a boy.* There is also mention of longer arbuda (embryo) for females compared to males.

The following items should be added to the diet in this trimester.

- Rice
- Goat milk or Goat cheese
- Vegetable soups (all vegetables)
- Pomegranate, sapote, guava, and apples
- Spinach and beets
- Amla candy
- Honey
- Pumpkin
- Figs
- Dates
- Ghee

At this time, from the fifth to the seventh month, the Kapha in the body increases. This means that weight gain will begin more rapidly now. The baby feels hungry. This means that the mother feels hungry. There are sharp hunger, pangs, and desires. The baby bump begins to show, and the mother might feel a little out of breath. Some women start experiencing incontinence at this time.

The last trimester

This is the trimester where you are preparing for the baby to arrive. This is the trimester when it becomes harder to walk normally, where you can no longer see your feet and can feel back pain, shoulder pain, and cramps.

Joints become loose in preparation for the baby. Women experience fake contractions called Braxton Hicks. They can also have constipation and digestive issues.

Eating small meals with digestive spices is vital at this time.

Massage and oil therapies are valuable. Self-massage is also essential. Massaging the breasts should be practiced daily before a bath. Massaging will help with itching, dry skin, relaxation, and stress.

Some Āyurvedic oils for massage are:

Vāta - Sesame oil
Pitta - Coconut or sunflower oil

The seventh month is important because the fetus becomes AWARE at this time. It is said that the fetus is connected to its mother and the divine at this time.

Listening to mantras, and meditation is critical in the seventh month.

Avoiding stressors is vital.

The eighth month is especially important from an Āyurvedic Perspective. We believe that ojas (immunity) is transferred from mother to fetus at this time. Adding good fats and nutrient-dense foods is therefore suggested at this time.

Perineum massage may be started in the eighth month a few times a week. In India, a gentle oil enema and perineum massage is performed regularly. Oil massage and salt baths can also be enjoyed.

See Recipes at the end of the book.

Post childbirth

The baby is placed on the mother's breast so that they hear the mother's heartbeat. The umbilical cord should not be cut until it has stopped pulsating. As long as it is pulsating prāṇa and immunity is still flowing to the baby. The maximum amount of immunity possible should be passed to the child.

Post childbirth remedies include a gentle abhyaṅga oil massage on the belly when the mother is ready, and abdominal wrapping. Most Asian cultures have practiced abdominal wrapping postpartum for thousands of years. Now even the western countries have followed suit.

There are many reasons for abdominal wrapping. The abdominal muscles and the entire pelvic floor is weak. From the Āyurvedic perspective, there is too much "air and space" after the baby is born. To reduce air and space, daily abdominal massage with appropriate dosha oil is helpful.

A popular treatment is the usage of castor oil packs. Abdominal massage should be followed by abdominal wrapping for the whole day (but not during night-time).

In India, we take a lengthy place of thick cotton and tie it around the belly. Nowadays, there are some fantastic readymade belly wraps available. Belly wrapping should be done for as long as needed. A young woman or an athlete will get her uterus back into shape a lot quicker than a slightly older woman.

Cleaning and hygiene of the genital area are especially valuable postpartum.

Using a small spray bottle that you can directly spray the vagina with is best. A vaginal douche kit is another option.

My formula is using organic rose water or filtered water in the bottle mixed with herbs like turmeric and neem. I have also been known to add dried aloe powder to the mix.

Turmeric and neem herbs are drying and support a natural antifungal and antibacterial environment. Turmeric is also anti-inflammation, which is critical during the postpartum period.

Fumigating with natural herbs like sage, guggulu, or camphor may purify negative energy and the atmosphere.

Some postpartum recipes are

- kitchari – rice and mung bean in a soupy format
- bhakta rice - cumin rice cooked with butter / ghee
- steamed vegetables (soft) with butter / ghee and turmeric
- fenugreek leaves with baked potatoes (kasuri methi)
- shatavari and turmeric golden milk
- cumin, ajwain and coriander decoction

(Subscribe to our youtube channel Ayurveda-courses-online-Austin. We keep on posting recipes)

Chapter 6: Introduction to Vāstu

You may have heard someone saying that I am not in the right headspace. You yourself may have said at some time, "I need some space," needing time away from a person, problem, or even a place.

Most women have a natural instinct for creating a beautiful space for themselves or their families. A home is a woman's pride and joy. This is why most of the interior design industry focuses on marketing to women.

In order to digest food, we need some space or break from eating. Thus we eat after a break of 4 or 5 hours. If we eat continuously, we will fall sick and won't be able to digest.

Similarly, we naturally want to sleep (a break from our senses) and seek solitude when confronted with problems. We seek space.

In order to heal or achieve the balance, we need the right space literally and figuratively. In ancient scriptures, this art of creating the right space that brings wellness, auspiciousness, and health to our home is called Vāstu.

Basically, Vāstu is translated as the art of placement by some. However, Vāstu is a whole lot more than that. Vedic scriptures or ancient texts mention Vedic sciences, including Sthāpathya Veda or architecture based on Vedic arts. This art has condensed into Vāstu.

An ancient form of Vedic architecture became condensed into Vāstu thousands of years ago. Vāstu then traveled to China and became Feng Shui. *(This is what we Indians mostly believe. Chinese may not subscribe to this theory. However, sthāpathya veda and ancient vedic architecture is mentioned in books thousands of years before Feng Shui became popular).*

Vāstu believes our homes and the land that they sit on are living entities and an extension of mother earth's energy and not just four walls where we live.

The interiors and exterior design of our home or apartment building, the land they sit on, the road they face, and their alignment on the earth's gridlines all affect our well being. If the house does not follow energetic laws defined by Vāstu, then it may cause bodily or mental imbalance and may also hinder our financial progress.

Āyurveda doesn't contradict medical science. We believe in all systems of healing.

Similarly, Vāstu does not contradict modern architecture. It just follows old rules while agreeing on some modern tenets of how homes are built in the 21st century.

Modern architecture evolved based on how humans live, work, and play, and that is the prime consideration along with maximizing light and space in a house or an apartment building.

Architecture creates buildings and homes based on how we live, work, and play. Architecture takes into consideration the climate of the place where we reside and whether it is a city, countryside, or suburban area. It also takes into account the cultural environment as culture also dictates how we live.

In India, many modern architects study Vāstu as any Indian who wants a home built wants to base it on the ancient principles of Vāstu. In a suburb in Dallas with a South Indian population, homebuilders have started using Vāstu principles as demand for a new Vāstu home is high, and Indians will pay a premium price for them.

Vāstu is based on aligning the home with the energy of mother earth. Houses must be aligned with the true north of the planet (give or take 10 degrees) and have four cardinal directions - North, South, East, and West.

It should be aligned with the magnetic north of the earth. The four cardinal directions result in eight yoni or critical orientations. These eight orientations are represented with an animal.

These are:

Direction	**Symbol**	**Element**	**Translates to**
East	Flag	Water	East facing the front door and home facing the east road is considered the most positive. The best direction for physical and mental healing, abundance, and wealth.
South	Lion	Earth	Physical discomfort and imbalances
West	Bull	Air and space	Gives material prosperity but also may provide some mental discomfort and inability to finish projects.
North	Elephant	Water	Wealth and abundance. The second best direction for the home's entrance.
Southeast	Smoke	Fire	Liquidity; liquid cash, fire element. Digestion. Best for dining, kitchen.
Southwest	Dog	Earth	Relaxation; best for office or master bedroom
Northwest	Donkey	Air	Represents movement. Exercise room. Garage.
Northeast	Crow	Water	Peace, spirituality, relaxation. Meditation room, altar, office

If the city you live in has a good layout, then the house will have a good influence also. The karma of the place you live — city, state or country — also has an impact on Vāstu.

When you have a square or a rectangular-shaped home aligned with true north, there is a matrix in three dimensions called Vāstu Purusha Mandala. Vāstu practitioners shorten it to VPM. Mother earth herself has a VPM that is laid out energetically on her.

Our home's VPM is laid out length, breadth, and width and mapped with the cardinal directions of the building. When the house becomes wholly aligned it is blessed with the energy of the earth, the sun, the moon and the five elements of air, space, fire, water, and earth.

The head of the Vāstu Puruṣa lies in the northeast and feet in the southwest. Placement and building of rooms are based on this Mandala. **See the image of a yantra at the end of this chapter.**

This is a link to my podcast on Vāstu Puruṣa and its origin story:

https://anchor.fm/narayana-ayurveda/episodes/What-is-Vastu-indian-feng-shui--Part-1-efsbmr/a-a2i0a9c

Alternatively you can use the shortened link https://bit.ly/3ie2vwg

Activity 5: Creating the right space for healing

Step 4: Cultivate new habits
Create an altar, change your diet, add herbs and ancient practices to your life.

1. Declutter the part of your house or room where you will meditate and invite healing inside.

2. Create a beautiful altar (see below).

3. Make that particular area inviting and beautiful to your taste.

4. Add incense or aromatherapy essential oils.

5. Add healing colors and yantras *(geometric mandala design that requests divine intervention)* on the wall or the altar. If you are uncomfortable with yantras, try a small lovely painting, wallpaper, wall decal, or even a piece of fabric that brings you joy. If you have a small space, just do this all on a tiny scale.

This area will be used for nurturing your intention via meditation, and will invite universal healing energies.

The whole world is made up of five fundamental elements - space, air, fire, water, and earth. These elements must align in an altar also.

Creation of an Altar

1. Rectangle or a square table

2. Glass bowl/vase filled with water representing the water element

3. Candle (regular or electric candle—any would do) representing the fire element

4. Fragrant flowers for offering

5. Crystals representing the earth element

6. Empty bowl or plate in the center representing space element. (offerings go here)

7. Yantras

Intention box or envelope should be placed in the empty plate then hidden under it. When the intention or desire is fulfilled it should be burnt.

Nurturing our desire and intention

We learned to create an intention and package it beautifully with the right colors and place in the northeast corner. Now that you have your altar, we need a deity to activate and amplify its power. We need to nurture your desire and intention for healing.

If you don't have an altar, I would strongly suggest creating a small space in your bedroom or somewhere in your home with less noise and distractions into a meditation space with an altar.

Yantra

A yantra is a geometric design that corrects energy in a building or a home. It invites divine or universal forces inside the house. If you search for yantra online, the first definition that comes up is a mystical diagram. However, a yantra is a lot more than a mystical illustration. It is where the invoked deities and energy come and reside. It can be made two dimensional as a drawing.

It can also be three dimensional. When creating a yantra, some common shapes are circles, triangles, and hexagrams. In addition, lotus petals are added on the side.

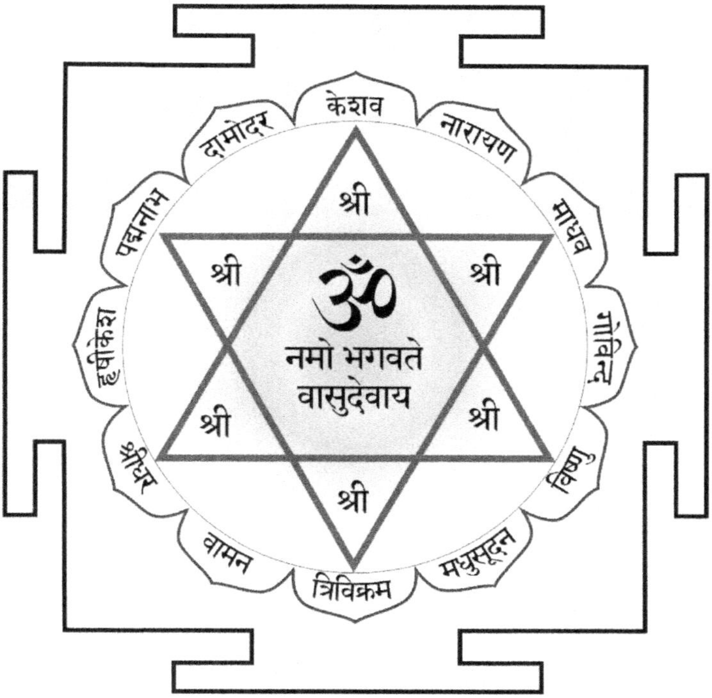

FIGURE 2: VISHNU YANTRA

Yantras can be used to manage or control imbalance in our life. They are used by Vāstu experts to manage and correct the spatial imbalance in a home or an office. However, they need to be activated first.

This five minute video shows how to activate Vāstu yantras:

https://youtu.be/JS8C189-IpQ

Chapter 7: Mantras and meditation

The power of sound

To activate the beautiful space, the altar we made, we need to use invocations and rituals to invite deities to amplify its powers. How do we do that?

Let's understand that mantras, chants or incantations - whatever you like to call them - are not something to be taken lightly. I have heard some ladies say, "Oh, I like the way it sounds, so let me start chanting this mantra." When I asked why, one of them answered, "because it sounds mystical."

One should not just chant any mantra for the heck of it. It's not a pop song. It can invoke good or bad energies. It can invite blessings if appropriately done, or invite the wrath of deities if done improperly.

Sound has power.

My spiritual master would talk about the power of sound a lot. He once said that when we speak hateful or critical words, they do not go in vain. They reverberate just like a ripple in a pond.

Similarly, if we use positive and sweet words, they are also heard and reverberated in air and space and water.

The most powerful sound are chants that glorify the Divine no matter what language, or religion.

In my ashram days, the chants that we learned had 16 syllables associated with the names of Krishna, the almighty, and we called it the great chant.

A chant can be repeated nonstop. Example:

Rāma, Rāma, Rāma, Rāma, Rāma.

Say that with the back of your throat. This is a chant.

In my role as a teacher of Āyurveda, especially when I am teaching nāḍī-parīkṣā (biofeedback from nāḍīs) or marma, the first order of business is to invoke the masters, gurus and higher power. It is followed by the activation of the student's third eye. I go around chanting on everyone's third eye and putting sandalwood offered to the divine in that area.

The teachers in our school and I will activate or reduce chakra activity via mantras.

Then, we go about our business of teaching Āyurveda.

Before I check someone's nāḍī or see a client, I also pray and do a little chant. This leads to many clients either surprised or asking me questions.

My beautiful students are always inquisitive, and this ritual attracts a lot of questions, curiosity, and seems mystical to them. My students are always asking me questions about learning new mantras.

The meaning of the mantra is considerably more profound than just an ordinary chant that helps calm the mind.

Mantra has become part of the English language but generally taken to mean an assertion that one may (sometimes mindlessly) repeat. However, that's not the case. Mantra can be translated as distinctive sounds that deliver the mind. Mantras have power and potency.

Mantras are sacred vibrations invested with divine power and will reciprocate with us as we respect them. They can also invite inauspicious and negative energy if done improperly.

In ashram life, we were also given these particular sounds called bīja or seed mantras. Seed mantras had seed words that could invoke the deity associated with that sound. These seed mantras could only be passed down from qualified Guru to disciple.

I used to think of them as "summon" mantras. These were the catalyst in increasing the power of our meditation and chants by orders of magnitude.

I wince every time I hear someone using the seed mantras, and I wonder if they received the mantra from a guru, or read it in a magazine.

Let's also clarify the difference between mantra and kīrtana.

Chanting and singing in a group loudly with instruments and music is kīrtana. In a kīrtana, we can also tell a divine story and glorify a diety. Many religions read their psalms, slokas, or holy verses in a chant-like poetic meter.

Kīrtana may be singing of sacred poetry and sacred books in a chant form as well. These chant forms are called "chandas" in Sanskrit. Think of it as a Vedic poetry meter.

There are six ways to recite Vedic chants. The shortest and most auspicious is called gāyatrī. The most famous example of this meter is the gāyatrī mantra from Ṛg Veda.

Coming back to mantras, there are many varieties, and they are meant to be invoked, or close a ritual. They may be a prayer, or asking blessing on a new house, or consecrating a new union, whether marriage or a business partnership. Mantras may be invoked to bless fertility and conception, or to bless a pregnancy.

There are thousands of mantras. If it helps, think of it as a chanting that is a common theme in many ancient religions, cultures, and regions around the world. From Gregorian chants to those recited by ancient Mayans, native Americans to songs of shamanic traditions - they invoke a higher power. Recitation of holy verses from spiritual texts may also be done in the form of a chant.

Chants can be spoken under the breath or loudly.

Think of it as an incantation that connects different dimensions and the realms - the gross physical world we live in and that which cannot be seen or perceived with our senses.

Let's start with the most basic.

At the beginning of this book, you saw a page with invocation mantras. These are called maṅgalācaraṇa. It means "auspicious beginning."

Usually, an invocation mantra begins with invoking the deity or higher power associated with our intention. If one has a spiritual guide or guru, they are also invoked at this time.

The altar that you created in the previous chapter is where the higher power will be invited to come and sit while you are meditating on them. To activate our altar and strengthen our intention, we should start with some invocation mantras.

As our altar is a "feminine divine" or "feminine angels" altar, we can invite mother earth, Śivānī, Lakṣmī, any of the female goddesses, or feminine angels.

Once we invite the angels or deities in our altar or home, we also need to ask them to leave. Usually, the end of the ritual is "Thank you for coming. Please come again. We are so grateful," followed by oṁ śānti śānti śānti. Let there be peace.

Invocations are done on an auspicious day like a full moon. They should be avoided on a Saturday as a general rule.

I have set out some examples of chants and mantras below.

Invoking feminine divine in your altar or garden

Even scientists agree that our planet earth is a living sentient entity. From the Vedic perspective, she is actually an incarnation of Lakṣmī, the wife of Lord Viṣṇu, the creator. Earth is His personal śakti or power.

In her personal form, she is a beautiful woman with four hands. She holds water, lotus, fruits (pomegranate), and vegetables and healing herbs in her hands. She can be invoked in the Northeast corner of your garden with a small fountain.

A sacred plant or a tree, or some scented flowers, can also be placed or planted here. A sacred plant includes Tulsi (holy basil), bananas, or figs. Scented flowers can be jasmine, honeysuckle, or gardenia.

As women, if there is one thing we can do to balance and bring healing into our lives, family, and community, it is connecting with mother earth.

A practical tip: I have seen people put up "fairy" gardens in so many places. Fairy gardens are very popular, and they are said to bring good luck and auspiciousness. Plus, gardens and plants bloom when the fairies are around.

From a Vāstu perspective, I advise my clients to put their fairy gardens in northeast corners, or near your mother earth corner of your garden. All the fairies are minions that serve mother earth. They would be very happy to have their goddess represented as well.

I don't have a deity of mother earth in my garden. My husband and I put up a little Koi pond, with water lilies, lotus, bananas, and other flowers as well as a fountain and birdbath. I also have my little fairies there, as well as other areas in the garden for protection.

We invoked the holy river Gaṅgā to come and reside in our small pond.

We also prayed over and around it, and invited mother earth in an energy form.

That little area attracts birds, bees, fireflies, dragonflies, and sees a lot of mystical activities. There will often be birds that are not regularly seen in city areas that will come to our little pond.

If you live in an apartment, create a miniature mother earth / fairy garden on a windowsill.

If nothing else, invoking mother earth in your home altar is also an option.

You will notice the word, devī. It means goddess or angel and denotes respect. We don't want to call them by name without using devī as a prefix or synonym. Just like we don't call our parents by name, we don't invoke the deities by name without using a respectful prefix or suffix.

(If you are afraid of chanting the mantras or getting them wrong, simply read it in English. Say it like you mean it. Let the words resonate in your heart).

Activity 6

Step 5: Cultivate new habits
Create an altar, change your diet, add herbs and ancient practices to your life.

In your garden or home altar

- Start the ritual by saying "I start the ritual."
- Invite Mother earth or any female deity by using these prayers and mantras below.
- Ask her to sit at the altar. (I have a small doll seat or a mini pillow to offer for sitting. Fairy garden decorative pieces work too).
- Offer her flowers in a vase filled with water representing water element.
- Offer her a candle (regular or electric candle —any would do) representing fire element
- Offer her fragrant flowers
- Offer her incense or essential oils
- Offer her a new dress. This could be a shiny beautiful piece of cloth from a craft store. Once she accepts it, keep it as her blessing to you.
- Offer your written intention and ask her to bless it.
- Offer her some food - fruits, juice, milk etc on a new plate or bowl that has never been used before.
- Thank her for coming.
- End the ritual by saying "I end the ritual," followed by and Om Shanti Shanti Shanti.

How to invoke the energy of mother earth and other feminine angels and deities?

Save the ritual flowers and cloth as a blessing for you. Repeat every full moon.

CHANTS

You don't have to chant in Sanskrit. Simply repeat the translation. Say it as you mean it. Say it loud. I will try to record this and put it on my website.

Bhūdevī mantra

समुद्रवसने देवि पर्वतस्तनमण्डले ।

विष्णुपत्नि नमस्तुभ्यं पादस्पर्शं क्षमस्वमे ॥

samudra-vasane devi parvata-stana-maṇḍale
viṣṇu-patni namas tubhyaṁ pāda-sparśaṁ kṣamasva me

Meaning:

Mother Earth, you wear the ocean as your blue garments, your bosom is the mountains. You are the consort of Lord Vishnu. I offer you my salutations and prayers. Please forgive me (and us humans) for any pain that we have caused you by our activities (as we walk upon you, touching you with our feet).

Lakṣmī Devī for abundance and wealth

Before the yantra is put on the wall, it has to be activated with a mantra and a ritual. Offer flowers, incense, and candle. Pray over it and invoke Lakṣmī via mantra in that drawing.

ādi-lakṣmi namas te 'stu para-brahma-svarūpiṇi
yaśo dehi dhanaṁ dehi sarvakāmāṁś ca dehi me

The prayer:

Mother Lakṣmī, you are the deity of all wealth and are all-auspicious. You are the wife of supremely powerful Śrī Viṣṇu. The world worships you as a deity of fame, wealth, money, and abundance. We are inviting you in the form of a Śrī Yantra (symbol of Lakṣmī) on the north of our home to attract your blessing. Please fulfill my intention. Please bless us and come and sit here.

Durgā Devī for relationship (seeking new partner/husband)

Durgā is mother nature. She is not mother earth, but nature personified. She controls sattva, tamas, and rajas in this world. If we think of the world as a home, she is the homemaker who organizes everything. She is the illusion potency. She is also worshipped by those who seek magic and illusion.

सर्वमङ्गलमाङ्गल्ये शिवे सर्वार्थसाधिके ।

शरण्ये त्र्यम्बके गौरि नारायणि नमोऽस्तु ते ॥

sarva-maṅgala-māṅgalye śive sarvārtha-sādhike
śaraṇye tryambake gauri nārāyaṇi namo 'stu te

Meaning:

You are the auspiciousness in all the auspicious, auspiciousness Herself, complete with all the auspicious attributes, who fulfills all the objectives of the devotees. O Gaurī, O Nārāyaṇī, please give me shelter.

Sarasvatī Devī before starting education

सरस्वति नमस्तुभ्यं वरदे कामरूपिणि ।

विद्यारम्भं करिष्यामि सिद्धिर्भवतु मे सदा ॥५॥

sarasvati namas tubhyaṁ varade kāma-rūpiṇi
vidyārambhaṁ kariṣyāmi siddhir bhavatu me sadā

Meaning:

I pray to you Devī Sarasvatī, giver of boons and fulfiller of wishes. O Devī, when I begin my studies, please bestow your blessings so I become capable of understanding and digesting knowledge.

The practice of meditation

When I teach meditation to students, I usually give an example of a famous actress in a famous movie who goes to India to "find herself." There is a scene where she is sitting in an ashram trying to meditate with one eye open, and her mind chatter prevents her from mindfulness.

The truth is not one serious meditation practitioner in India meditates like that. We practice first. We warm-up. We practice. We don't do it in a group for starters when we are beginners. Let me give you an example.

Let's say person A wants to compete in a marathon in 10 months. She will find a personal trainer. They will create a plan. Every day, at the same time in the morning, person A will put on her training clothes. She will start her day with an intense warm-up routine, then go running 3 miles for one month, then 6 miles in month 2.

In six months this person A will be running half the marathon distance, and as the marathon comes close, she will run the full length. This training will include meeting with a personal trainer and coach, following a strict diet, and giving up alcohol or junk food.

The idea is that once we have an aim and objective, we then build up our stamina to go further in our athletic endeavors week by week, month by month. We have a plan, and we practice a lot.

We always start with a warm-up.

Similarly, to meditate, first things first: you need to set a goal. Why do you want to contemplate?

Meditate is a state of trance that can put you in a state of bliss.

It is a state of non-thinking and non-feeling yet observing and feeling and thinking. It is a state of DEEP focus. It is a state where we can really see inwards into our souls.

Once the goal is set, a time limit is needed. A coach is required. You can also set short goals. I want to meditate for 10 minutes every day this month and build it to 20 minutes in two months. What time will you do it? Early morning is usually the best time. If you are not a morning person, try night when everything is quiet.

Before starting to meditate, a warm-up is needed. Yogic breathing exercises called prāṇāyama are the best way to warm up before a meditation. Chanting or kīrtana music is also another terrific way to warm up.

Choose the method that works for you.

Dress the part.

Loose-fitting light colors in natural fabrics are the best.

Take a scented bath.

Light a lovely candle or try some ambient lighting and essential oil.

Sit very comfortably either on a cushy chair, sofa, or couch. If you can handle sitting on the floor on a yoga mat, even better.

You can also put on classical music without lyrics. (I find lyrics may be distracting).

Activity 7

Remember the six steps:

1. Become the observer
2. Acknowledge what you observe
3. Create intent
4. Cultivate new habits
5. Work on the mind. (Body follows)
6. Surrender

As part of step 4 and step 5, we will cultivate a new habit and work on our mind by having a daily meditation plan-even if its 5 minutes a day.

Step 5: Work on the Mind (Body follows)
Step 6: Surrender

Now you are finally ready for Step 5 and Step 6. We will work on our mind and surrender. We will begin with some breathing exercises.

Warm-up:

Breathe in, hold the breath, and breath out for a minute.
Alternate nostril breathing for another minute
Regular, but deeper breathing for another minute.
Now, run a scan from top of your head to your feet, taking note of any discomfort.
Put your tongue on your palate and chant OM a few times.

Invocation

Invoke your deity, or a higher power at this time to help you meditate.

Touch your third eye chakra with your ring finger (any hand) and ask your spirit guide or deity to open your third eye.

Put your hands on your heart center and now look within.

Stay in this looking state, observing your spiritual, inner self for one minute on day one. (make it two minutes the next day, three minutes the next and so on).

If the mind starts to chatter, simply repeat the breathing exercise. It should temporarily stop the mind chatter.

Ingredients for meditation

- Pillow or couch or comfortable chair OR a yoga mat
- Incense stick or essential oil
- Comfortable clothes
- A timer (you want to start with 5 minutes or less in the beginning and slowly increase it every day)
- Altar (if you made an altar for your female diety, this is the best place to meditate)
- Nice music (classical cello, Tibetan bells, Om or soothing chants but no lyrics please)
- Self help meditation from any audio provider may also help. (optional)

The object of meditation

Meditation is not done in a vacuum. It is a deep contemplative state on a place, person, pastime, event, vision. Meditation has a focus, a goal. Without defining a focus for our meditation, our session will be as good as useless.

Meditation in the modern world has taken many connotations- rumination, contemplation and reflection are part of this practice now.

According to Vedic scriptures called Upaniṣads, meditation means becoming calm and concentrated, to look within, and to perceive yourself within oneself.

Verses from ancient scriptures have highlighted that meditation without an object of meditation will not give a permanent benefit.

However, when used with sound, correct mantras, regulated Āyurvedic practices that enhance the flow of prāṇa, meditation can support mental, physical, and emotional imbalances.

The ancient Vedic scriptures make it clear that meditation can not only elevate us as spiritual beings living in a human body but also help to prevent and heal imbalance. Meditation can bring positive changes to the physical body and mind, which is the center of emotions. Meditation can help dispel negative thoughts.

Example

Visualize a lush rainforest garden with no dangerous animals. It has giant trees with juicy fruits and fragrant flowers. There is a waterfall. On a beautiful chair, Mother Earth is sitting in a personified form. You can see a lot of young servitors attending this Gaia in a green and gold dress with flowers in her hair. Blessings and light flow from her to you.

This is an example of visualizing a place or a person.

ACTIVITY 8

Morning or evening when you have some quiet time, do this five minute meditation

Sit in a quiet place on a comfortable chair. You can also sit by the altar that you created. You can choose to light an incense or use some natural essential oils. Listen to the sound of bells or nature.

Say the following words:

My body is a temple, the mind is my altar, and my soul needs to love and give. This can be recited aloud or whispered to yourself.

I honor myself. I respect and love myself.
Please let me accept what's favorable to my body, my mind and my soul.

I honor myself, I thank myself and I will treat my body and mind with the same respect I show in a place of worship.

I SURRENDER to the feminine Divine.

"My body is a temple, the mind and heart are my altar, and my soul along with divine resides in this altar. I will love and respect my temple, and altar and treat myself with respect. I will practice ahiṁsā towards myself and others and be more tolerant and grateful for this temple."

Chapter 8: Communing with nature through herbs

Mother earth has given us this beautiful thing called plants. Plants are producers; they produce food, and we are consumers of this food. We get our nourishment and healing from this production. Mother nature procreates life in the form of plants.

She has a womb, and all seeds grow into plants, fruit trees, vegetables, flowers and healing herbs year after year, season after season. As a woman, our feminine side demands a connection with nature, plants, and herbs to stay in balance. We don't need to be a herbalist or a great chef to do that.

Nature, the feminine Divine, can be honored in several ways.

Let me start by explaining first what an herbalist is, and what is the difference between a western herbalist and an Āyurvedic herbalist. We will then talk about how you can become an avid user of herbs.

In the west, when we think of herbalists, we mean a person who studies herbal medicine, botany and uses plants for therapeutic uses. Western herbalism includes dietary supplements. A western herbalist may create teas, infusions, salves, tinctures, oils, vinegar, jams, etc. It is understood that an herbalist should be able to cultivate herbs, be an avid gardener, and has studied anatomy and holistic pathology. She should be able to create formulations or suggest herbs for supporting myriad ailments.

Āyurvedic herbalists, though similar in their skill set, may wear many more hats. First and foremost, an Āyurvedic herbalist first needs to be an Āyurvedic practitioner. I consider myself a Vedic herbalist who also happens to be an Āyurvedic practitioner.

Traditional Āyurvedic herbalists used mantras, harvesting rituals, and more traditional gardening and herbal practices to commune with the feminine Divine. I will try to teach some of it to you through this book. It is not possible for me to grow all my herbs, but I try to work with whatever I can. When we were buying our house, our biggest concern was the kitchen and having a garden to plant and grow herbs.

Honestly, this love of herbs and communing with nature at a deep level with mantras and rituals cannot be taught — it is lived.

The million-dollar question is, can you use ancient Āyurvedic healing practices without using plants and herbs?

The answer is no. Herbs and plants alongside these healing practices are integral to balancing our feminine side.

I once had a client (let's call her Joan) whose husband dragged her to see me. She had lost 70 pounds in one year and was merely 90 pounds due to IBS. She told me she "hates, hates, hates" shopping for food, cooking it or eating it, and in particular, she hated vegetables.

I told her then that food hates her right back. If we are directing such hateful energy towards mother earth's babies, she is not going to like it. Plants, vegetables, and produce is a blessing from mother earth. We don't have to like it. But we mustn't dishonor this manifestation of her maternal energy.

Joan had no appetite and just had lost all her taste for food. I gave her the homework of going and looking at the produce section of an organic grocery store (only looking and asking for forgiveness). I also gave her Chyavanprasha (Āyurvedic tonic), and really small amounts of a decoction made up of cumin (Jirakarishtha) with some pomegranate juice.

She called me really late at night within the next week and informed me she was really hungry. In less than a week, her appetite had fully returned.

I have had many clients ask me how they can practice Āyurvedic herbalism for themselves and for their community. I love teaching moms and women about herbs. They will then teach their own mothers, sisters, friends, and daughters.

If you teach a woman, you show her entire family.

What are the tools at our disposal?

We can buy seeds, dried herbs, and readymade kitchen spices - see the list below. Choose whatever works for you. Please don't feel you have to invest in everything.

- Flowers: Rose (powdered), rose jam, jasmine tea, hibiscus tea
- Roots: Turmeric root powder, dry ginger powder, fresh ginger root, fresh turmeric root
- Fruits: Pippali (long pepper), cloves, black pepper, dried mango powder (amchur), dried pomegranate powder
- Seeds: Fennel, cumin, coriander, fenugreek, onion (kalonji), ajwain (yavani), black cumin
- Leaves: Fenugreek (kasuri methi are the dried leaves. Fresh fengureek leaves called methi are also available from time to time in Indian grocery stores), Tulsi, curry leaves, bay leaf, cilantro, mint
- Bark: Cinnamon
- Pods: Green cardamom pods, black cardamom pods, vanilla
- Resin: Asofoetida (hingu)

You can also grow some essential herbs that you buy from your local home improvement store to put in your windowsill or verandah. Make sure it is near your kitchen and accessible to you.

If you are going to awaken your inner goddess and instill a lifetime of healing practices, you must learn to be in contact with mother nature and mother earth. The best way to do that is by growing or taking care of plants, especially herbs. It is also a beautiful way to destress.

If you don't have a garden, having a few herbs or a few flowerpots in your windowsill is more than enough.

I once had a client whose husband passed away. It had been a few years, but it was apparent a lot of her health issues were because of her inability to destress. As a younger woman, she had been a keen gardener. Now, she lived in an apartment. I encouraged her to do some windowsill and porch gardening in pots and pans. Plus, I asked her to cook with Āyurvedic herbs and spices.

She canceled her last appointment with me and wrote to me that she was feeling so much better by connecting with nature again, that most of her stress-related symptoms had disappeared.

That is the power of herbs (and doing something we love).

Clean one windowsill in your home or apartment that gets good light.

If you have a garden or a raised bed or can manage some potted herbs - even better.

Some potted plants that can be grown from a well-lit windowsill include basil, parsley, cilantro, dill, oregano, rosemary, sage, and thyme. Start with one or two herbs first, or those you find tasty.

Don't bother growing them from seeds. Just buy them ready-made and transplant them.

As you spray water every few days on the leaves, invoke mother earth in your home, your life, and she will respond if you are sincere.

Herbs like oregano, cilantro, basil should be harvested every few days.

If you have a hot summer, try getting a curry plant. Curry leaves love hot weather but do not like winter (when the temperature drops below 40 degrees Fahrenheit). I usually take my curry leaf inside in the winter or simply grow it annually.

You can also invest in cheap annuals like marigold that not only repel insects but help other herbs as well. Marigold is an IMPORTANT flower. It is favored by angels and goddesses along with jasmine, gardenia, and honeysuckle (the latter are hard to grow and can be expensive — but marigold is cheap, annual and requires less attention comparatively).

Marigold is used for offering in our rituals. Dried marigold flowers are used for making salves and so on.

Also, invest in glass jars and spices for your kitchen cabinet. I prefer that my clients and students buy spices as whole seeds, as they better retain prāṇa or vitality. However, if you want to invest in storing a powdered spice, focus on making it airtight and keep it away from sunlight.

If you are not going to be growing any herbs, at least invest in a small coffee grinder and use it as a spice grinder to make your own powdered spices. We call mixtures of powdered spices churnams.

Āyurvedic herbalists also use animal-based products like honey, ghee, feathers, conch shell, dried coral, and even crystals and gems.

Using honey, ghee, feathers, and crystals in a ritual is also part of our healing routines.

Using mantras and invocations when you harvest your leaves or flowers will increase the efficacy of the herbs.

Offering fresh herbs in a ritual to goddess earth will bring abundance. Post ritual, dry the herbs and flowers and either put them in a jar or create a tea or make a churnam out of them. (see below).

Most western gardeners do not have auspicious practices surrounding the act of harvesting these plants, and the workers who are paid to help collect the herbs may not be in the right frame to contribute to its efficacy according to traditional Āyurvedic practices.

Herbs in ancient cultures, as well as Āyurveda, were used in the following forms.

1. Cool infusions - 1/2 cup dose
2. Hot Tea - 1-2 cups a day
3. Decoction - 1/4 cup
4. Juicing - 1/2 to 1 cup depending on the doṣa (vāta, pitta or kapha women have different needs)
5. Pastes, jams or confectionaries - small amounts. Let's say enough to spread on toast.
6. Cooked in ghee – for example, garlic or ginger fried in ghee
7. Cooked in oil (topical)
8. Mixed in beeswax as balms
9. Tablets called vatis (cooked in ghee and then dried)
10. Boiled in milk – for example, golden milk
11. Jams - see pastes. For example, rose jam, amla jam, pumpkin jam, fruit jam with herbs.
12. Candy - amla candy, ginger candy, licorice candy
13. Naturally fermented wines (āsavas and arishtams) (contraindicated during pregnancy)
14. Herbs infused with power of the sun and agni (kept in glass container in a window facing the sun in the east for a day)
15. Herbs infused with power of the moon or soma (kept in glass container in a window facing full moon)

One main missing component of the Western administration of herbs is the vehicle. Most herbs are taken in capsule form with room temperature or cold water, which can also reduce the efficacy and absorption compared to being paired with the appropriate vehicle for the reason of application.

Even in Āyurveda, an herb can be taken with a glass of water. If boiled in water, it is a decoction. If infused in hot water, it is tea. If soaked in cold water, it is an infusion. Water is a universal solvent, and we ask clients to take their herbs with warm water, or as teas or decoctions. However, we use other oil-based, honey-based, alcohol-based solvents also. We call them anupānas.

In Āyurveda, any substance, edible or not, that gives us healing is called a dravya.

Water may be boiled and put in the sun to absorb sunshine. Such water has heat increasing quality and is easy to digest. Water that has been boiled and cooled, then put in the rays of the full moon all night has a cooling and peaceful effect. Similarly, herbs processed in an iron vessel may increase heat, herbs kept in a silver container may become cooling, and so on.

In the west, we want to focus on extracting active nutrients and botanicals for medicinal uses. In Āyurveda and ancient cultures, mostly the whole herb was used. Extractions are avoided.

Some vital women support herbs are listed below.

- Lotus seeds (tridoṣik)
- Rose (yes, eating dried rose jam) (tridoṣik)
- Fenugreek (vāta, kapha)
- Ajwain seeds (vāta, kapha)
- Shatavari (phytoestrogen)
- Walnuts (vāta, kapha in small amounts)
- Soy (for vāta only)
- Grassfed cow milk (vāta, pitta only)
- Ghee (vāta, pitta only)
- Sesame (vāta, pitta in very small amounts)
- Sunflower (kapha and pitta)
- Pumpkin (cooked) All doṣas
- Pumpkin seeds - All doṣas in small amounts
- Turmeric
- Ashwagandha
- Punarnava
- Musta
- Vidari

- Cumin
- Coriander
- Fennel
- Ginger
- Sandalwood (pitta)
- The essential oil of rose (vāta, pitta, kapha)
- Dried Pomegranate seeds
- Pomegranate molasses
- Pomegranate jelly
- Rose jam
- Rose syrup
- Rosewater
- Aloe vera
- Castor oil (for warm packs topically, and for massage)

Herbs suggested for vāta

To Balance Energy

Herbs: Ashwagandha, Tulsi tea, licorice, dashamula

To Balance Digestion

Herbs: Cumin, coriander, asafoetida, ajwain, ajmoda, fennel seeds, triphala, haritaki, cumin corriander fennel (CCF) tea, fenugreek tea

Herbs for Pitta

General Herbs: Fennel, coriander, cardamom, saffron, parsley, fresh basil, rosewater, ghee.

Skin: Neem, turmeric, manjishtha, mint, rosewater, amla berry

Also: Buttermilk, probiotics, dried pomegranate skin powder, pomegranate molasses

To Balance Digestion

Herbs: Ajamoda, ajwain, fenugreek, long pepper, ginger, black pepper, triphala, cumin, coriander, fennel, licorice, tulsi, ginger, black pepper

Teas: Ginger tea, licorice tea, tulsi tea

Also: Buttermilk, probiotics, lassi with trikatu, ginger kashaya, ripe bilva fruit powder, dried pomegranate skin powder, pomegranate molasses

Chapter 9: Ancient wisdom and modern nutrition

Western nutrition advocates a certain number of calories, protein, vitamins, and minerals based on the weight of a person. It doesn't give importance to where this nutrition comes from: pills, frozen, canned, or dried food.

Western nutrition advocates for eating two portions of vegetables and fruits per day. Again, in this pretext, the source of the fresh produce is not a consideration; it is widely believed that you can get your daily servings from any fruits and vegetables regardless of how they were harvested or stored.

It doesn't matter if the groceries are organic or conventionally grown, genetically modified, frozen, canned, tinned, or dried.

In contrast, Āyurveda places a profound significance on where your food grows, when it is harvested, and whether any harmful and biologically significant pesticides were used. Sometimes, chemicals are used to change soil acidity. They may harm the soil health in the long run. Soil health and organic, biodynamic farming is vital to Āyurveda.

Focus is on where and how the food was grown and harvested. Organic, fresh, and local fruits and vegetables are preferred. Canned, tinned, frozen, and other conventionally grown foods are to be avoided. (whatever and however is viable)

Āyurveda also believes overeating or undereating, eating the wrong combinations (raw with cooked, or milk with fruits), or eating late at night can disturb agni.

Agni is the digestive fire. If not taken care of, a disturbed digestive fire will become a causative factor for a future imbalance.

The purpose of food is not just to keep the body functioning and healthy, but also to keep the mind pure, and our spiritual potency flowing, to keep us connected to the universe and the Divine.

The purpose of food is to increase our lifespan, and to balance our mind and emotions as well. Think about it, will a double cheeseburger, fried food with 900 calories, white bread with no nutrients, a dead body of an animal, and a processed cheese balance your mind and emotion? It will not even give nourishment. We are stuffing ourselves with empty calories night and day!!

Overcooking the food or spicing it up to such an extent that the flavor is lost in the process kills the prāṇa in the living foods as well.

Avoid eating meat, flesh – especially red meat – as much as you can.

We get physical, mental, and energetic nourishment from the food we eat, from our thoughts and senses, and from the air we breathe. Our environment also influences and nourishes us. In Āyurveda, nutrition is referred to as āhāra, meaning that which sustains us. Thus breathing is included as part of our sustenance.

Ancient Vedic teachings suggest that we receive most of our nutritional needs from an actual fresh plant-based diet, ideally organic and grown locally.

In addition, Āyurveda believes in the principle of preserving health by putting in our body only those things that are compatible with our doṣa, which do not harm our digestive fire, and are easy to digest.

Food is the first medicine. If we are eating the right foods, we don't need medication. In fact, many food items and herbs (kitchen spices) as well as herbal Āyurvedic formulations cross over. For example, Āyurvedic jam with amalaki may have ghee, honey, many herbs, and food supplements.

Below are some helpful suggestions that you can use to regain your power along with your emotional and physical balance.

Buy prāṇa infused local produce

The first injunction of a Vedic diet is to use local produce. Buy as local as possible. This ensures that the product has vitality. It is a living food.

Mother earth is a living person. What she produces is living produce with vitality and her divine energy. We can taste this vitality in freshly harvested tomatoes or strawberries. We call it prāṇa.

Offering living prāṇa infused produce to your body – food that is fresh, organically grown vegetables, fruits, and unprocessed whole grains fills us with prāṇa. It's best for healing.

The nature of food that is produced is directly affected by the climatic conditions and how it was grown.

Some years ago, one of my students was complaining that it was snowing on the east coast, and she didn't have access to the local fruits, vegetables, rasas, and grains to balance herself. I suggested she use seeds, whole grains, and dried fruits that had been produced locally. Seeds and whole grains retain vitality and prāṇa.

I agreed with my student. Access to freshly grown produce is a real problem in some parts of the country.

In some rural and small towns, the residents have to travel long distances even to get conventionally grown vegetables, never mind fresh organic, and local food. Luckily, organic farms nowadays produce beautiful organic foods in colder climates. This means people living in extreme winter conditions don't have to go without fresh produce.

What if you are preparing food and there is 10 inches of snow outside? Where will you find local foods?

The solution in a cold climate is to dry and preserve local produce for the winter. Jellies, jams, pickling, and drying herbs for teas are some of the methods available. This does reduce prāṇa. However, it also gives us a way to preserve local produce.

Another example of a food that retains prāṇa for years are seeds, beans, nuts, and whole grains (not powdered and milled grains but actual grain berries like wheat berries, or rice).

A student once asked me what is better, local or organic? Obviously, both local and organic is the best. But if I had a choice between conventionally grown Texas peaches from Fredericksburg, really close to where I live, or organic peaches from another country — I will choose those delicious, Texas-grown peaches hands down.

Those Texas peaches were exposed to the same harsh summer as I was. It should be okay to eat locally for most people when consumed in moderate amounts.

Where do frozen foods and leftovers fit in?

Some years ago, I was supporting someone who had Multiple Sclerosis through pañca-karma and Āyurveda. He had switched over to more plant-based foods from a meat and potato diet. He kept asking me if organic frozen peas and vegetables are okay to cook, and I kept saying no. That was frustrating for someone who had already made such a significant change.

Foods that are leftovers or are frozen have no energetics, and are subject to laws of time and karma.

There is karma associated with time. When time passes, the law of nature is that food must start decomposing even if something is in the fridge or in cold storage (we are not talking about nutrients but prāṇa and the subtle energetics of healing)

According to the laws of nature, everything decomposes and recycles. Energetically, once we cook fresh produce, it begins to lose prāṇa. It begins to decompose gradually, even in the fridge, within 3 hours of being prepared. *(Bhagavad-Gītā)*

If the food is animal-based, it starts decomposing the minute the animal dies and the soul leaves the animal's body. Eating such foods will increase our state of tamas and rajas energy, affect us mentally, and hinder our healing process if we are unwell.

If we want to use food as a healer, we cannot be eating things that are in the state of decomposition, nor can we eat something that has 100 chemicals added to prevent decay. We need to eat more fresh plant-based foods.

We cook it, add spices, and eat it fresh. Simple.

Sattva, rajas and tamas diet

According to principles of Āyurveda, foods that are refined, laced with chemicals and additives, are leftovers, frozen, or stored for a long time are to be avoided.

They will not just cause allergies and irritate our GI tract in the long run, but will also affect our mind.

Rājasika foods like onions, garlic, mushrooms, can energize us. However, overindulgence can affect our minds.

An animal-based diet will increase the qualities of lethargy and ignorance. (rajas and tamas). Such foods may be rich in protein, but they also carry harmful energy stored from the fear and emotions of the animal when it was killed. They are also devoid of prāṇa.

A plant-based diet is the best diet. However, if you are unable to do it, follow a mostly plant-based diet by percentage, and limit and reduce animal-based foods.

When we buy processed foods, they have been laced with additives and all kinds of chemicals that take them away from their natural state of purity or sattva, away from what used to be real food.

Plant-based diet

Favor a more plant-based diet at least 75% of the time if you want to get maximum healing results.

Recently, I saw a documentary in which someone was trying to look for the perfect human diet.

However, if we look at the premise of Āyurvedic medicine, which claims that every single human being is unique and has a unique psycho-physical constitution (doṣa) - how can a perfect diet exist? It does not. It cannot!

An ideal diet does NOT exist. It must be customized. Period.

A diet must be individual to the person, her constitution, age, environment, state of her health, mindset, the seasons, and where she lives.

A beneficial Āyurvedic diet for pitta is lacto-vegetarian. If my clients cannot handle it, I ask them to do a plant-based Āyurveda diet Monday to Thursday, and they can indulge in some animal-based foods on the weekend. Even that little change brings vast benefits.

A beneficial diet for the vāta body type is mostly plant-based with some animal-based products (such as dairy and eggs). However, all food must be cooked. I ask vāta clients to follow an 80:20 split of plant-based and animal-based if they can't see themselves as vegetarians. A vegan diet is not suggested for vāta women.

The best diet for kapha is mostly vegan, except for small amounts of honey, buttermilk, and goat milk.

If I have clients that can manage a switch to a plant-based Āyurveda diet, the benefits certainly outweigh the negative.

This certainly doesn't mean we are asking you to be 100% vegetarians. However, to strive for this diet is ideal. Even a 75% plant-based diet for your body constitution will change and transform your physical body, heal your soul, heal your mind, balance your karma, and connect you deeply to mother nature and the Divine.

Such a diet is mostly situated in sattva. It advocates freshness, purity, and healing intention. The idea is to avoid tāmasika foods that may affect the mind adversely.

A regulated doṣa pacifying diet with six tastes is preferred. The six taste groups are as follows:

- Sweet: Earth + Water
- Sour: Earth + Fire
- Salty: Water + Fire
- Pungent: Fire + Air
- Astringent: Air + Earth
- Bitter: Air + Ether

Taste	Examples	Doṣa
Sweet (as found in nature)	Whole grains like whole wheat and barley; fruits like mango, banana, pineapple, watermelon, and dates; and cow's milk	Best for vāta and pitta. Kaphas should avoid these rich nurturers.
Salty (as found in nature)	Natural salts, sea vegetables, mineral water	Best for vāta
Sour	Citrus (lemons, oranges), tamarind, yogurt, fermented foods	Best for vāta
Astringent	Dried beans like kidney beans, navy beans, legumes like mung beans, pomegranates, dry bananas, strawberries, blueberries	Best for pitta and kapha
Pungent	Onions, cayenne pepper, raw garlic, mustard oil, radish, horseradish, daikon	Best for kapha
Bitter	Dark leafy greens like chard, rhubarb, kale, bitter melon, unsweetened dark chocolate, chicory	Best for pitta and kapha

Sometimes my clients, especially in Texas, associate vegetarian food with bland vegetables and vegan food with tofu.

I don't blame them. I am from India and was also perplexed when I saw that most vegetarian people in the United States sustained on tofu-based products. I don't even like tofu, and, being a kapha body type, it also doesn't suit me.

No wonder my clients are put off the minute I mention that in order to detoxify, they will have to incorporate a more vegetarian diet!

Āyurveda has such tasty and delicious recipes that you will never go back to bland food and store-bought hot sauces.

Importance of detoxification

Detoxify at least once a month, and for one week each in spring and fall.

For a woman, it's essential to fast especially around the new moon or no moon, for the moon affects her menstruation cycle as well as her emotions. However, detoxifying once or twice a month is suitable for most well persons.

We work from Monday to Friday and give ourselves a two-day break. Why don't we give that break to our stomach, our colon, and our GI tract? Why do we expect our stomach, kidneys, and liver to work 24/7 – 365 days a year – without any break, and overload them with processed food, chemicals, and harmful substances?

We also need to give our digestive system a break. Fasting on fruits or vegetables and on simple broth soups once every two weeks is ideal.

You can just have water, vegetable juices, rice, and mung bean soup.

The best time to detoxify is the juxtaposition of seasons - spring and fall.

If it is hard for you, try to fast on days that suit you!

Once you know your doṣa, select the Āyurvedic recipes best suited for vāta, kapha, pitta, or recipes that are warming, nourishing, rejuvenating, depleting or detoxifying.

Offer prāṇa infused living foods to your body. Treat this temple with respect!

- **Nurturing** yourself means eating foods that bring comfort. Good fats are the best nurturers. Example: sesame seeds, flax seeds, chia seeds, almonds etc.
- **Eat vegetarian** as much as possible.
- **Cook yourself** as much as you can. Even if you have time only to make yourself tea twice during a day, just do that with love.
- **Cook with love** and think positive thoughts while cooking.
- **Celebrate eating** together – savor the food that was cooked with love as well as the company.
- **Eat slowly,** savoring every bite. Don't spoil it by eating while watching TV, working on the computer, or riding in the car. At least one meal a day should be eaten slowly.
- **Eat living foods** – Living foods are full of prāṇa – eat organic as much as possible. Fresh – Farm fresh if possible – for they will increase the prāṇa or Chi in your body. Such foods will heal you, rejuvenate you, and help you find the balance you have lost. We lose balance in many ways such as overeating, eating too much pasteurized food or microwaved food, or eating on the go.

Do note that the advice I give as an Āyurveda practitioner in the stories I share is not medical advice. Āyurveda practitioners cannot treat, prevent, or diagnose any disease. Our clients come to us for information and suggestions. They may or may not use some ancient wisdom of their own accord. It is totally up to them.

Case Study

Twenty-two-year-old Sheila (name changed), after being vegetarian most of her life, became a meat-eater during her college years due to the lack of cooking and vegetarian options in England.

Coming from India, she had never been exposed to processed foods, slices of bread, or the array of junk food growing up. According to her, she grew up on a wholesome Āyurvedic balanced diet.

However, due to lack of time, the stress of juggling school and job, an unhappy relationship, and growing isolation, Sheila turned to junk food as her companion. Her weight grew by 60 pounds in one year. She was always bloated and constipated.

In the beginning, her body rejected the mistreatment she was giving it but eventually got addicted to it. She says she didn't know how to stop! She also developed fibrocystic breasts during this time, and her periods were painful and heavy.

Her face turned sallow, and her face was bloated and swollen. People mistook her to be in her forties.

Her Āyurvedic practitioner suggested she find an apartment with a kitchen. Sheila started eating a home-cooked vegetarian diet suitable for a kapha person with agni increasing spices like ginger, pippali, black pepper, cayenne pepper, and turmeric.

Her Āyurvedic practitioner made bitter, scraping Āyurvedic decoctions for her to lose weight and encouraged her to chant and sing kīrtana and do meditation sessions to balance her emotional isolation.

Sheila was also suggested to start offering her food to the Divine with mantras.

As soon as Sheila turned strictly vegetarian and started accepting whole grains, fresh fruits and vegetables, and started empowering the food with mantras, two things happened immediately. She lost the weight, all of it, and her mind became calm. Her grades at school improved.

Her constipation, bloatedness, and menstruation issues finished.

Case Study 2

Vinetta (name changed), was referred to me by a chiropractor. She had acute digestion issues, chronic constipation, and dependence on laxatives. She also had some hormonal issues.

She was a vāta body type, had no allergies, and had recently developed a slight sensitivity to milk and wheat. She noticed she felt heavy and bloated every time she consumed animal-based foods, dairy, or wheat. Laboring with chronic constipation, she had been taking laxatives and enzymes to move her bowels. She also had back pain.

I determined that her vāta and kapha were imbalanced.

According to Āyurveda, kapha energy is sensitive to milk and wheat to start with (Not lactose or gluten intolerant -- but may have some sensitivities). These are considered heavy.

From an Āyurvedic perspective, overdoing dairy and whole wheat every meal had sensitized her internal kapha system.

When nature has given us a variety of grains – amaranth, quinoa, buckwheat, millet, barley, brown rice, etc. we have still ended up eating wheat a lot more than other grains. It is something that many of us find hard to give up, especially in the form of bread or pasta.

Maybe it's cultural. In Japan, Vietnam, and many South Asian countries, it's mostly rice with every meal. In North India, it is all about whole wheat - because we grow it. The rest of India loves different varieties of rice.

In Mexico, it's corn and wheat. In America, it is whole wheat stripped of everything; bleached till it is nothing but an empty calorie bulk food (then with artificially added vitamins on the top of it, since we have stripped it of nutrition to start with).

When I suggested a temporary, plant-based diet that slowly phased out milk and wheat gluten for a month, the expression on her face was one of horror.

I suggested a vegetarian, practically milk-free, soy-free, gluten-free diet for a few weeks. Along with this diet, I suggested that she reduce sweets, salt, and citrus fruits for this month.

She could have 1/2 cup of organic non-homogenized, organic milk only in her coffee once a day. The rest of her diet would be a variety of grains – amaranth, millet, quinoa, barley, brown rice, mung bean flour, wild rice, garbanzo bean flour, beans, and farm-fresh green leafy vegetables. We also stopped her sweet fruit intake. (According to Āyurveda, kaphas are naturally prone to unhealthy sugar metabolism, and can quickly become pre-diabetic).

The Āyurvedic herbs Triphala and Trikatu, a multi bitter herb formulation, was suggested.

For her food preparation, we suggested cilantro, coriander seeds, fennel seeds, and cumin – all considered natural digestives, as well as asafoetida (I taught her how to prepare the food, and, gave her recipes).

Within weeks, her dependence on laxatives reduced. She was going to the bathroom every single day like clockwork. Her skin glowed, she was full of energy.

The problem for Vinetta was how she could maintain the diet after the initial month was over. So, I asked her to eat an 80:20 Plant: Animal ratio in her diet. Her cheats and heavy to digest foods were only suggested during lunch, making a dinner a more straightforward affair.

Eating at lunchtime, when the sun is at the highest increases our digestive fire.

Eating the same food at night, when the digestive fire is low – may lead to heaviness the next morning.

So, it's not just what you eat, but when you eat it and how you prepare it.

Chapter 10: Yoga for Women

Yoga has become so mainstream in America that it is the object of jokes in movies, and many scenes are filmed in a yoga setting.

A person who practices yoga is expected to be fit and thin and do lots of body bending. This is the dire opposite of what yoga is.

Yoga is for everyone. Yoga is NOT āsana (pose). Āsana is only 1/8th of yoga practice.

Yoga is meant to be practiced by anyone, whether five years old, 15 years old, 25 years old, or 80 years old. The idea is to practice what you can - breathing exercises or simple poses. You do whatever is possible for your mind and body at that time.

My first experience with yoga was in fifth grade, where yoga was a 45-minute weekly class. We took the exams, and we gave presentations. It left a lasting impression.

Yoga is a personal practice. Looking at the mirror, admiring ourselves, and competing is not the point. Who can do a pose better is counterproductive. When I first came to San Diego from Delhi, I joined a gym.

I was in culture shock in the yoga class. I was in loose cotton clothes. Everyone else was in their designer yoga clothes and checking each other out in the mirror. This was not a personal practice.

I finally found a real teacher. My beautiful friend and yoga teacher, Sudevi, who was a true yogi. Even though I did not learn from her long, she left an impact on my practice. *(The exact term is yoginī for female yoga practitioners. However, the term yogi has become so mainstream I will go with it).*

My advice to most of my clients is to look for an experienced and yoga teacher who will work with you and has been practicing yoga for a long time. Find a teacher whose energy complements yours. That's a tall order for some states.

Focus on your teacher, not the studio.

So, what is yoga, and who is a yogi?

In the west, a yogi is simply someone who goes to a yoga class regularly, is possible a semi-vegetarian, and may or may not meditate. If your friend does yoga as exercise and does not follow any other limbs of yoga, then she is not a yogi.

According to Yoga Bhāṣya, which is the oldest commentary on Yoga Sūtras of Śrī Pātāñjali, a yogi may be a beginner in the path of self-realization or someone who has reached a certain level and aims to reach enlightenment by the end of this lifetime.

Nāḍīs: Energetic channels of our body

For this chapter, I have focused on some yoga āsanas for our energy centers. These energy centers are called chakras. Some of you may be familiar with the seven energy centers.

Did you know that all of us have both masculine and feminine energies in varying proportions?

Our left side is associated with feminine energy
Our right side is associated with male energy

To understand chakras, we first need to understand three energetic waves that flow in the left and right sides of our body.

- This dynamic wave that flows from the left is called Īḍā Nāḍī.
- The energetic wave that flows from right is called Piṅgalā nāḍī.
- The energy that flows from our spine is called Suṣumnā nāḍī.

The meeting points of these channels are called chakras. These spherical energy centers are nexi for the circulation of these male and female energies in the body. The function of the chakras is the circulation of Chi or prāṇa.

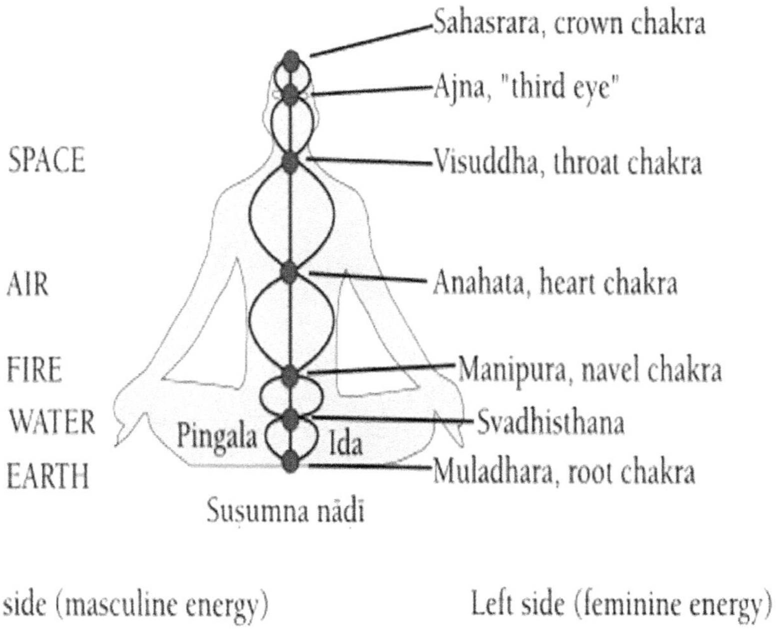

The seven chakras

1. Sahasrāra chakra is located at the crown of our head and supports our pineal gland.
2. Ājñā chakra, in the center of our eyebrows, is wisdom, intuition, our third eye.
3. Viśuddhā chakra, in our throat, supports communication, speech, and inner hearing.
4. Anāhata chakra is our heart chakra. This energy center is full of love, kindness.
5. Maṇipura chakra is located behind the umbilicus.
6. Svādhiṣṭhāna chakra is the sacral region. It is associated with sexual pleasure, reproduction, adrenal glands, and kidneys.
7. Mūlādhāra chakra is the root of the spine. It affects reproductive organs, excretion, and colon

Āsanas

In the following section, there are yoga poses for each of the seven chakras or energy centers given for information purposes.

Please DO NOT do any exercise or yoga pose without talking to your health care advisor. If you have never tried yoga before, seek an experienced yoga teacher, or a yoga studio with experienced teachers (not someone straight out of yoga teacher training). Look for a studio where you find a mix of classes for different levels.

Starting with a restorative yoga class, or hatha yoga with props for beginners is usually a good start. A yoga teacher in a yoga studio will assist your āsana, guide you, and may give you one on one attention.

However, in most traditional gyms, the yoga teacher is not allowed to assist or touch the yoga class participant.

These poses should not be tried without the help of a teacher. They should all be modified to your ability. Use props like pillows, yoga blocks, and chairs. Most importantly, always warm up and always ask your yoga teacher for help.

Below are pictures from a traditional Vedic yoga studio by an experienced yoga teacher and an Āyurveda practitioner who used to be my student.

Traditional yoga studios are called yoga shalas. When you google a studio, use the keyword “yoga shala” for better results.

Crown chakra

Crown chakra is significant when you feel ungrounded. Working on the crown and root chakra (last chakra) supports and grounds us to mother earth.

It helps our vāta or when we feel scattered. Most important, this chakra is essential for clarity and insights.
Headstand is the best pose for this chakra. However, most of us cannot do it. Below is another option.

Forward Fold: You can use a pillow or a yoga block, so the top of the crown chakra is resting on those blocks.

Model: Pradeepa Rayasam

FIGURE 3 FORWARD BEND (CROWN OF HEAD SHOULD TOUCH THE FLOOR OR A BLOCK)

The "third eye" chakra

This is beneficial when you have been spending too much time in front of the TV or a computer.

A lot of mental activity overstimulates our third eye. Rubbing our hands and putting on top of our eyes and third eye help deactivate the third eye. Chanting Om also helps the third eye.

Most balancing poses focus on this energy center. The idea is when we balance, we "fix" our gaze on a point. That fixing of the gaze during the balancing is what activates and balances this chakra. You could also do a simple version of standing on one leg and focusing on the wall. That also works!

FIGURE 4 BALANCING POSES

FIGURE 5 BALANCING POSE 2

Throat chakra

Talking requires energy. Ask any teacher or singer. If you have been talking all day, or not talking at all, or if you have high or low throat energy, this is the chakra we need to support.

This chakra is associated with communication, speech, and intuition.

Chanting OM from the back of the throat, breathing from the end of the throat, and the following poses help the throat chakra.

Notice any pose that extends your throat, and the upper body helps your throat.

FIGURE 6 COBRA POSE

FIGURE 7 WHEEL POSE

Heart chakra

Our heart chakra is the center of our emotional energy. It is the most important center for our emotional health. Physically, it supports lungs, blood circulation, respiration, diaphragm, and thymus gland.

Every time you yawn and extend your arms, you are opening your chest. All chest openers and backward bending poses support the heart chakra.

Stomach chakra

This chakra is associated with the organs of our abdomen and digestive power. It is associated with pitta energy.

All the spinal twists work on this energy point, support vitality, reduce heat and intense emotions.

Sacral chakra

The sacral chakra supports all that resides in the sacral area.

It is associated with sexual pleasure, reproduction, adrenal glands, and kidneys.

Forward folds and forward bending poses strengthen this chakra.

FIGURE 8 FORWARD FOLD

Root chakra

The root chakra is vital for grounding our energy. It grounds us physically and mentally.

It is located at the root of the spine.

This root chakra supports the pelvis, reproductive organs, excretion, and colon.

All the hip opening āsanas work on this energy center.

Questionnaire

ACTIVITY: Let's find out our Natural and current constitution

Instructions:
Column 1: prakṛti (original constitution, manifest during childhood years and early teen years)

Answer for when you were a teenager

Choose on a scale of 1 to 5 *(1 being the lowest and 5 being the highest. If it doesn't apply to you, leave blank)*

Column 2: Vikṛti (current constitution)

Answer for the last six months

Choose on a scale of 1 to 5 *(1 being the lowest and 5 being the highest. If it doesn't apply to you, leave blank)*

Fill ALL three questionnaires twice. Add all the points.

The form where you get the highest scores is your dominant constitution/dosa.

Inputs: Heather Thomas

Vāta woman profile

Qualities of vāta: dry, light, cold, rough, subtle, mobile, clear

Vāta	Original Constitution Age 12-15 years Answer for when you were a teenager Choose on a scale of 1 to 5, *1 being the lowest and 5 being the highest. If it doesn't apply to you, leave blank*	Current Constitution (In the last year) Answer for the last six months Choose on a scale of 1 to 5, *1 being the lowest and 5 being the highest. If it doesn't apply to you, leave blank*
Structural Qualities Skinny, thin, and tall; or short, wiry bodies. Hard to gain weight. Weighing less than BMI standards. Small to medium size eyes. Bony wrists and cheekbones are often visible. Thinner hips than pitta counterparts. Hair is thinner as well.	1 2 3 4 5	1 2 3 4 5
Functional Qualities Dry hair, dry skin, dehydration, and constipation. Vaginal dryness.	1 2 3 4 5	1 2 3 4 5
Digestive Snapshot A tendency for bloating, constipation (Hard, dry stools).	1 2 3 4 5	1 2 3 4 5

Severe Nausea during pregnancy Appetite is sometimes dull or non-existent		
Mental Profile Learns easily, forgets easily. Creative intelligence – art projects, music, dance, theater, etc. Naturally intuitive when balanced. When imbalanced, manifestation of anxiety, phobias (fear of different things). May become emotionally ungrounded, constantly worrying. May exhibit lack of focus and not able to stick to projects.	1 2 3 4 5	1 2 3 4 5
Menstrual Cycle Menstrual cycle may become irregular. Light bleeding 1-3 days The blood itself may be dark reddish sometimes. There may be additional bloating, and/or constipation at this time Low backache is usually common Cramping (a lot of pain if a person is imbalanced, less if they are balanced) Pain in hips/legs	1 2 3 4 5	1 2 3 4 5
PMS Feeling spaced out, mood swings, anxiety, and worry. However, this is temporary	1 2 3 4 5	1 2 3 4 5
Pregnancy and Post Partum There is not a massive amount of weight gain during pregnancy. Even if it does happen, it comes off easily. A tendency to be anemic during	1 2 3 4 5	1 2 3 4 5

pregnancy. Fatigue, anxiety, worry, and constipation during pregnancy Postpartum, you may have difficulty nursing, or there may not be enough milk. (if imbalanced.)		
Menopause All of the above qualities are exacerbated. Worry, stress, anxiety, feeling spaced out. Osteoporosis is more common in vāta menopause. (Tendency to be low in estrogen)	1 2 3 4 5	1 2 3 4 5
ADD ALL THE NUMBERS IN THE NEXT COLUMN		

Pitta woman profile

Qualities of Pitta: hot, sharp, light, liquid, mobile, oily

Pitta	Prakṛti (original constitution) Answer for when you were a teenager Choose on a scale of 1 to 5 *(1 being the lowest and 5 being the highest. If it doesn't apply to you, leave blank)*	Vikṛti (current constitution) Answer for the last six months. Choose on a scale of 1 to 5 *(1 being the lowest and 5 being the highest. If it doesn't apply to you, leave blank)*
Structural You are medium size in clothes, medium build. If you go by BMI, your BMI is usually close to what is advised by the medical community. (Vātas are usually thinner than BMI or underweight, and kaphas usually heavier or overweight)	1 2 3 4 5	1 2 3 4 5
Functional Pitta will usually show as excess heat in the body - fever, migraines, hot flashes, thirst, fainting Skin issues (acne, psoriasis, dermatitis)	1 2 3 4 5	1 2 3 4 5
Digestive Snapshot Strong digestive systems Excess loose stools, indigestion and heartburn if overactive.	1 2 3 4 5	1 2 3 4 5

Mental Profile Quick and sharp minds, learn easily with a great ability to concentrate and understand. Leaders or managers Wise and opinionated at the same time. Critical, judgmental, quick to anger, critical and perfectionistic.	1 2 3 4 5	1 2 3 4 5
Menstrual Cycle Hot flashes Excess blood flow Bright red in color Long periods (10 days) Acne (heavy breakouts) Sharp cramping Headaches / migraines Diarrhea	1 2 3 4 5	1 2 3 4 5
PMS Irritation and anger Skin breakouts Anxiety, insomnia	1 2 3 4 5	1 2 3 4 5
Pregnancy Able to have good energy during pregnancy. Can feel hot and temperamental Nausea/vomiting and acid reflux Tendency to control the pregnancy Post partum, both vāta and pitta go out of balance. Dehydration is common during and after pregnancy.	1 2 3 4 5	1 2 3 4 5
Menopause Scorching HOT flashes Temperamental Angry	1 2 3 4 5	1 2 3 4 5
ADD ALL THE NUMBERS IN THE NEXT COLUMN		

Kapha woman profile

Qualities of Kapha: heavy, slow / dull, cold, oily, liquid, slimy/smooth, dense, soft, static, sticky/cloudy, hard, gross

Kapha	Prakṛti (original constitution) Answer for when you were a teenager Choose on a scale of 1 to 5 *(1 being the lowest and 5 being the highest. If it doesn't apply to you, leave blank)*	Vikṛti (current constitution) Answer for the last six months Choose on a scale of 1 to 5 *(1 being the lowest and 5 being the highest. If it doesn't apply to you, leave blank)*
Structural Kaphas may or may not be overweight, but their bones and body frames are larger and stronger. Luxurious thick hair, skin, and nails Kaphas are usually heavier or overweight compared to the standard BMI (Body Mass Index) Gain weight easily but they have a hard time losing weight	1 2 3 4 5	1 2 3 4 5
Functional Excessive water buildup in the body results in water retention, weight gain, colds, congestion, and respiratory	1 2 3 4 5	1 2 3 4 5

allergies. Heavy / slow qualities like fatigue & excess sleepiness.		
Digestive Snapshot Their appetite is consistent, and they tend to have slower digestion and metabolism. They have excellent health and strength and tend to live long lives.		
Mental Profile They are generally calm people who love to sit in contemplation, do nothing and sleep. Kapha people have deep stable faith and compassion for others. They are slow to anger. While it takes a longer time to learn new information, their memory retention and recall is excellent. Kapha people can suffer from laziness and attachment issues including greed and possessiveness.	1 2 3 4 5	1 2 3 4 5
Menstrual Cycle Lasts 3-5 days Heavy breasts Water retention Dull pain	1 2 3 4 5	1 2 3 4 5
PMS Feeling sentimental and lazy Heaviness in breasts Slow metabolism Wanting to cry		

Pregnancy As a general rule, kapha women have the best pregnancies. Their symptoms are milder and their energy is higher; however, they tend to become very slow to move at this time.		
Menopause Weight gain, fluid retention Swelling breasts Emotional, crying Lethargy, laziness	1 2 3 4 5	1 2 3 4 5
ADD ALL THE NUMBERS IN THE NEXT COLUMN		

Āyurvedic kitchen

Some must-have spices for your kitchen

Cumin, coriander, fennel, cardamom pods, cinnamon sticks, nutmeg, allspice, mustard seeds, dried pomegranate seeds, sesame seeds, pumpkin seeds

Buying and storing spices

- Purchase from a reliable vendor. Stay away from cardboard packaging.
- Look for organic, non-irradiated spices that are as fresh as possible (check use-by dates).
- Remove from plastic containers and store in airtight glass or tin containers.
- Whole spices have a much longer shelf life and carry better flavor for longer
- Ground spices go stale fast (after 6 months – and that's with optimal storage).
- Avoid light, heat, moisture, and air (encourages the evaporation of spices' volatile oils).
- Store in a dark, cool place (ideal temperature is 50-60F). They don't need refrigeration.

Cooking with spices:

- Dry roast or roast in ghee or oil
- Add seeds first (cumin seeds, fennel seeds – don't burn them!)
- Add dried and fresh spices second (dried leaves, herbs, fresh ginger).
- Add powdered spices last (powdered cinnamon, powdered turmeric).
- Add the fresh ingredients last. It's okay to add the powdered spices with the fresh ingredients.
- If using cardamom, add it last

Cumin Recipes

- Sip the warm water boiled with cumin throughout the day- eases bloating and cramping.
- Milk boiled with cumin supports lactation.
- Cumin powder can be used in soups and stews.
- Cumin powder can be used with fresh homemade buttermilk to support digestion.

Fenugreek

- Fenugreek tea
- Soak fenugreek seeds in water overnight and eat the seeds in the morning. Alternatively, drink the fenugreek infused water.
- Roast and powdered fenugreek and cumin for increasing lactation.

Ginger

- Ginger tea
- Ginger candy
- Crystallized ginger
- Chew a small piece of fresh ginger with a tiny pinch of salt.
- Use fresh ginger in soups and chutneys.

Turmeric

- Add turmeric to different curries.
- Use it in the preparation of khichari.
- Use it in mung dal soup.
- Add a pinch of turmeric to warm milk.
- For a vāta, turmeric with ghee is beneficial

Fennel

- Fennel tea (digestive rasayana with cumin and coriander).
- Churnam with other spices to use in food preparation.
- Chew roasted seeds after meals as a digestive aid.

Goals of Āyurvedic Cooking

1. Select local produce appropriate for the current season.
2. Cook using fresh food and eat soon after cooking.
3. Cook consciously and hygienically.
4. Buy whole seeds rather than powdered spices
5. Plan your shopping trip; always have a list.

Useful Cooking Techniques

• **Stir-frying**: Heat ghee or oil, add spices, add veggies, cook gently with a lid until cooked.

• **Boiling**: Cook with boiling water. Either let your food (dal, veggies, potatoes, rice) absorb water, or discard the rest. Alternatively, you can save this broth water for further use.

• **Pan roasting**: Place veggies in a covered Pyrex dish with some oil or ghee and roast in an oven

• **Frying**: Cook in hot oil or ghee

• Combination of the above cooking techniques (boiling followed by stir-frying, etc.)

- Ginger decoction
- Golden milk
- Rooiboos chai
- Ojas "warm" smoothie
- Laddu (women's support sweet balls)
- Popped lotus seeds

Ginger Decoction

1 Tbsp grated ginger
2 cups of water

Boil water.
Add Ginger.
Let it boil till the water reduces to 1 cup.
Cool it down. Mix with tea or almond milk.
Sweeten it for taste if you like.

Digestive support, Nausea Support

Golden Milk

1 tsp Turmeric
1 tsp crushed cardamom pods
1 cup organic whole milk (or alternative milk if you prefer)
pinch black pepper
pinch nutmeg
pinch saffron (optional)

Date syrup OR Rose sugar/jam

Boil milk
Add turmeric, black pepper, and saffron.
Bring to boil.
Cool it down.
Sweeten it for taste if you like.

Two sweetener options:
rose jam (cooling and supports moods)
date syrup (to increase immunity and iron)

Golden Milk: Fatigue support, immunity support, kapha increasing, vata and pitta pacifying.

Women's support sweet balls (Laddu)

1 cup garbanzo bean flour
2 Tbsp ghee
1 Tbsp raw sugar (traditionally unrefined cane sugar called guda is used)
2 Tbsp seeds:
 Pumpkin, sunflower mix (Pitta / Kapha)
 Sesame, chia, flax (Vāta)
For taste either:
 Cardamom or
 Vanilla

Heat a pan and add garbanzo bean flour (besan)

Dry-roast garbanzo bean flour, stirring continuously.
After a minute or two, add ghee and mix well.

Continue cooking until garbanzo bean flour begins to turn a golden nutty brown. Do not overcook.

Add sugar and mix well till all sugar is dissolved and it makes a paste. Add Vanilla or cardamom for taste.

When it can be rolled over, take it off the flame.

Scatter the seeds on a plate.
Roll the paste onto it. Now roll it in balls.

In India, we call this laddu.

Popped lotus seeds (makhanas) snack

- Pinch salt
- Pinch lemon seasoning
- Pinch fresh lemon
- Pinch fenugreek powder
- 1 tsp sugar
- 1 tsp Ghee

Add ghee to a hot pan.

Add 1 cup readymade popped lotus seeds
Add the spices. Mix well.

Pour fresh lemon juice and sprinkle some cilantro on top.

Supports reproductive health and increases ojas. Pregnancy support. Lactation support

About the author

Monica B. Groover is an Āyurveda practitioner, teacher, respected author, and herbalist.

Ms. Groover comes from a heritage of Āyurveda, Vedic astrology, and herbal healing. Her father was a famous Vedic astrologer and herbalist in India.

Ms. Groover has been teaching Āyurveda in the United States for the last 12 years.

She has prepared Āyurveda curriculum for graduate courses and different Āyurveda colleges.

A music buff, advanced meditation practitioner, and herbalist, Ms. Groover practices and teaches traditional Āyurveda. She is the director of an Āyurveda school in Texas and also previously founded an Āyurveda college in San Diego, California.

She practices energy medicine and Vedic healing through mantras.

A NAMA (National Ayurvedic Medical Association) member at the Āyurveda Doctor level, Ms. Groover's research, and articles have been published in peer-reviewed journals. Ms. Groover is in the process of finishing a textbook to help Āyurveda Counselor students.

Ms. Groover also served NAMA (National Ayurvedic Medical Association) as a board member in 2018-2019. She continues to serve on different committees with NAMA, including the standards committee, exam committees, etc.

Printed in Great Britain
by Amazon

82777533R00130